EVERY PERSON'S
GUIDE TO
JEWISH PRAYER

EVERY PERSON'S GUIDE TO JEWISH PRAYER

RONALD H. ISAACS

JASON ARONSON INC.
Northvale, New Jersey
London

This book was set in 12 pt. ITC Garamond Light by Alabama Book Composition of Deatsville, Alabama.

10 9 8 7 6 5 4 3 2 1

Library of Congress Cataloging-in-Publication Data

Isaacs, Ronald H.
    Every person's guide to Jewish prayer / Ronald H. Isaacs.
       p.   cm.
    Includes index.
    ISBN 0–7657–5964–0 (alk. paper)
    1. Prayer—Judaism.   2. Judaism—Liturgy.   I. Title.
BM669.I83   1997
296.4—dc20   96–41190

Manufactured in the United States of America. Jason Aronson Inc. offers books and cassettes. For information and catalog write to Jason Aronson Inc., 230 Livingston Street, Northvale, New Jersey 07647.

*Rav Anan said: The gates of prayer are never closed,
as it is written (Deuteronomy 4:7): "For what great
nation has a God so close to it as Adonai our God is to
us, whenever we call upon Him?" And what is calling
upon Him, if not prayer, as it is written (Isaiah 65:24):
"Before they call, I will answer; while they are yet
speaking, I will have heard."*

*Another interpretation: "Let my prayer come before
You, Adonai, in a time of love and favor" (Psalms
69:14). This means that a person who prays alone must
hope that the time of prayer is an acceptable one. But for
the prayer of the congregation, there is never an unac-
ceptable time. Thus, it is written (Deuteronomy 4:7):
". . . whenever we call upon God".*

—Deuteronomy Rabbah 2:12

CONTENTS

INTRODUCTION

Prayer is the natural expression of people's religious feelings. In the Jewish tradition, prayer has always occupied a prominent position of importance. The Bible records the personal and often spontaneous prayers of the great men and women in the early history of the people of Israel.

The development of congregational worship is a distinct contribution of Judaism to the other faiths that sprang from it. Over the centuries, with the emergence of new synagogues whose local customs often reflected the local culture, new prayers were written and added to the existing liturgy. Prayer, especially of the communal variety, continues to be the Jew's way of communicating with God. The prayerbook continues to define the moral and ethical concepts that lie at the core of Judaism.

Of all of the activities with which Jews as a people have been concerned, perhaps nothing is more impor-

tant and less understood than prayer. Many people are
confused by or uncomfortable with prayer because they
are unfamiliar with the liturgy or cannot read Hebrew.
Many modern-day worshippers, unfamiliar with the history of the prayerbook and the origins of the prayers, fail
to be moved by even the English translations.

   The goal of this book is to introduce readers to some
of the basic concepts of Jewish prayer. It presents an
array of facts and customs related to the language of
prayer and the prayerbook, the historical development
of prayer and the prayerbook, various genres of prayer,
prayer garments, some of the major concepts of the
important standard prayers, notable prayer quotations,
and a glossary of prayer terminology and concepts. It is
my hope that this volume will help the reader to feel
more "at home" with the prayerbook, the Jewish concept
of prayer, and the prayerbook's many ethical and religious teachings. Additionally, if this book provides a
basis for future reading and the impetus for readers to
emerge in further study on the subject of prayer, I will be
most gratified.

                                        Ronald H. Isaacs

WHAT IS PRAYER?

I have poured out my soul to the Lord
—1 Samuel 1:15

Prayer is the attempt to establish a conversation with God. The Greek word that translates to "to pray" means "to wish" and the French word means "to beg." The English word means to entreat, implore, or ask earnestly. The Hebrew word *l'hitpallel*, usually translated as "to pray," is derived from a word meaning to "judge" or "assess." For the Jew, prayer is a way of relating to ourselves, to our fellow human beings, and to God. Prayer provides us with an opportunity for reflection and self-examination in order to consider who we are and what we should become.

It is interesting that the Mishnah (*Baba Kamma* 2a) uses as a synonym for "human being" the word *mav'eh*, which the Talmud (*ibid.* 3b) derives from the foot, *ba'ah*, meaning "to pray." Thus, according to the rabbis, a human being is, by definition, one who prays.

In the Bible, there is a commandment that states, "You

shall love God with all your heart, soul, and mind"
(Deuteronomy 11:13). The rabbis interpreted the service
of the heart to refer to the act of prayer. Thus, for the
Jew, prayer becomes a *mitzvah*, a religious obligation.

Many different types of prayers exist: petition, thanksgiving, adoration, and praise. Although Judaism encour-
ages its people to be content with its lot, it does not
expect that lot to be stagnant or petrified. Prayers of
petition express our desire to improve our lives.

The measure of a person's happiness is limited only by
one's capacity for gratitude and appreciation. Prayers of
thanksgiving are meant to evoke appreciation in worshippers and to remind them to concentrate on what
they already have, rather than on what they do not have.

In prayers of adoration and praise, we consider the
majesty, greatness, and mystery of the Divine. Singing
praises to God is the Jew's way of honoring God for His
greatness.

The Jewish prayers, for the most part, are written in
the first-person plural, because the Jews, as a people,
have been intensely conscious of themselves as a group.
Indeed, the watchword of Jewish solidarity is found in
the talmudic statement that "all Israelites are responsible
for each other" (*Sanhedrin* 27b).

BEFORE WE HAD FORMAL PRAYERS: SACRIFICES

The Biblical Period

The Hebrew word *korban* (sacrifice), meaning literally
"to bring near" or "to approach," occurs some eighty
times in the Bible, especially in the books of Leviticus

and Numbers. A sacrifice was, therefore, a means by which to approach God. From the dawn of human history, the sacrificial offering was the basis of divine worship. Sacrifices were generally offered to obtain God's favor and to atone for the sins of the sacrificer. They also demonstrated one's submission to God and served as a formal recognition of God's great power. Although human sacrifice was practiced by some ancient cultures, it is strictly forbidden by biblical tradition. The Bible forbids offering a child to Molech (Leviticus 18:21), and the account of Abraham's attempted sacrifice of his son Isaac (Genesis 22) and God's intervention strongly suggests that human beings were never meant to be sacrificed.

The first sacrifices recorded in the Bible were offered in Genesis 4:4 by Cain ("fruit of the soil") and Abel ("the choicest of the firstborn of his flock"). Noah made an offering (Genesis 8:20ff) that the Bible describes as having a pleasant odor. Sacrifices were also made at various local shrines, such as Beth-El, Shiloh, and Hebron. Many of these had been Canaanite shrines that the Hebrews took over upon settling in the land. In the Book of Leviticus, all forms of magic and incantation were banished from the sacrificial cult.

Although the libation of wine and meal offerings played a prominent role in some of the rituals, the most important biblical sacrifices were animals. The sacrificial animal had to be wholly unblemished, domesticated, and the property of the person making the sacrifice.

The sacrifices can be divided into various categories: propitiatory and dedicatory offerings, meal offerings, libation offerings, fellowship offerings, thanksgiving offerings, free-will offerings, and ordination offerings.

Propitiatory Offerings

Two offerings belong to this category: the sin offering, called *chattat*, and the guilt offering, called *asham*. The sin offering was suited to the rank and circumstance of the person who offered it. Thus, the High Priest would bring a young bull (Leviticus 4:3); a *nasi* ("ruler") would bring a male goat (Leviticus 4:23); and a commoner would bring a female goat (Leviticus 4:28) or a lamb (Leviticus 4:32). A sin offering of one male goat was required on each of the sacred festivals: the New Moon (Numbers 28:15), each day of Passover (Numbers 25:22–24), Shavuot (Numbers 28:30), Rosh Hashanah (Numbers 29:5), Yom Kippur (Numbers 29:11), and each day of Sukkot (Numbers 29:16,19).

Rites of purification called for lesser sin offerings. For example, lambs or birds were offered after childbirth (Leviticus 12:6–8), leprosy (Leviticus 14:12–14), or unclean issues (Leviticus 15:15).

The guilt offering was a special kind of sin offering (Leviticus 5:7) that was required when someone was found to have been denied his or her rightful due. The guilty party had to bring a guilt offering, usually in the form of a ram. The guilty person also had to confess his or her sin and make full restitution plus twenty percent (Leviticus 5:16–24). If the wronged party was no longer alive and there were no survivors, the payment went to the priests.

Dedicatory Offerings

This category of sacrificial offering reflects the more universal concept of offerings in general. Emphasizing the surrender of the gift to God, the dedicatory offerings represented the act of commitment that followed the repentance expressed by the sin and guilt offerings, thus opening the way for the communal sacrifices that often followed.

Burnt Offerings

An *olah*, from the Hebrew word meaning "to go up," used the following animals: bulls, sheep or goats, and birds (Leviticus 1:3–17). A continual burnt offering (called an *olah tamid*) was made twice daily during biblical times. It consisted of two male lambs that were sacrificed, one in the morning and one in the evening (Exodus 29:38–42). Two additional lambs were offered each Sabbath (Numbers 28:9–10). No sin offerings accompanied the burnt-offering sacrifices; on the other hand, a sin offering of one goat was required along with the burnt offerings on the other holy days. Bulls, lambs, and rams were the animals primarily used for the burnt offerings.

Various purification rituals also called for burnt offerings: childbirth (Leviticus 12:6–8), unclean issues (Leviticus 15:14–15), and hemorrhages (Leviticus 15:29–30).

Meal Offerings

Regularly accompanying the animal sacrifices was the meal offering (*mincha,* in Hebrew). The meal offering generally consisted of a mixture of fine flour, oil, and frankincense, and often took the form of baked loaves or wafers. The meal offering usually accompanied each burnt offering, and its quantity was generally fixed according to the animal being sacrificed. Meal offerings were rendered after such joyous occasions as the cleansing of a leper (Leviticus 14:10) and the successful consumption of a Nazirite vow (Numbers 6:15). No meal offering accompanied the rite of cleansing after childbirth or unclean issues.

Libation Offerings

A libation (*nesech*, in Hebrew) normally accompanied both the burnt offering and the peace offering (Numbers 15:1–10). The libation, a drink offering of wine, was considered an additional "pleasing odor" offering (Numbers 15:7), and the amount of wine used depended upon the type of animal being sacrificed. Libation offerings were mentioned in the Bible in connection with the Sabbath (Numbers 28:9), the New Moon (Numbers 28:14), Shavuot (Numbers 29:18), and Passover (Numbers 28:16–29).

Fellowship Offerings

This category consisted of those offerings that expressed a voluntary desire on the part of the offerer. With few exceptions, they were not required by explicit rules, but were permitted on the condition that the sacrificer had met the requirements of penitence. As an additional expression of devotion, it was permissible for a burnt offering to accompany the fellowship offering.

Peace Offerings

Called *shelamim* in Hebrew, the peace offering was the basic sacrifice of all communal sacrifices. Any domesticated animal was permitted for use as a peace offering, which always concluded with some type of communal meal. The peace offering was specified for only the celebration of Shavuot (Leviticus 23:19–20), the ritual for the completion of a Nazirite vow (Numbers 6:17–20), and the installation of the priests (Exodus 29:19–34). National events that called for the peace offering included the successful completion of a military campaign (1 Samuel 11:15), the end of a famine (2 Samuel 24:25), and the praising of a candidate for the kingship (1 Kings 1:9).

Thanksgiving Offering

Known in Hebrew as a *zevach*, this is the most frequently mentioned type of peace offering (Leviticus 7:12–13). In some instances, the peace offering and the thanksgiving offering are synonymous (e.g., Jeremiah 17:26).

Wave Offering

Known in Hebrew as a *tenufah,* the priest's portion of the peace offering was "waved" before God, an act that demonstrated that the offering belonged to God. The waving was only a preliminary to offering up the animal or meal offering on the altar fire (Exodus 29:24,26).

Votive Offering

Called a *neder* ("vow") in Hebrew, this was usually a peace offering, but sometimes a burnt offering. An example of a votive offering was the vow of a Nazirite that was consummated by a peace offering (Numbers 6:17–20).

Free-will Offering

Called a *nedavah,* this was the minimum offering that could be brought to the holy convocations that took place on the three Festivals of Pilgrimage. Like the votive offering, it could be burnt in addition to a peace offering (Leviticus 22:17–24).

Ordination Offering

This type of offering, called *milluim* ("to fill the hand"), was used to consecrate a person to God's service (Exodus 28:41). The details of the ritual are spelled out in Exodus 29:19–34, where Moses acts as the officiant of the ordination of his brother Aaron and Aaron's sons.

The Second-Temple Period

During the Second-Temple period, sacrifices were offered almost exclusively in the Jerusalem Temple. The Temple's sacrificial service basically followed the order prescribed in the Bible, except for the addition of a water libation on the festival of Sukkot. The talmudic tractate *Tamid* discusses in great detail the sites, times, and kinds of sacrificial offerings held in the Temple. The high point of the sacrificial service was the two daily offerings—the *tamid* offering at daybreak and the other in the afternoon—that began and concluded each day's service. All of the other public and individual sacrifices took place in between.

A most interesting system was devised to allow for public representation at the Temple's sacrificial ritual. The priests and Levites were divided into twenty-four shifts of duty that took turns at officiating at the Temple sacrifices. Each watch was responsible for one week's tour of duty every six months. The country was divided into twenty-four districts, and each district appointed a delegation of pious Jews to represent it at the public offerings. The men chosen for this delegation were known as the *Anshay Ma'amad* (Men of Standing) because they stood by to observe the Temple ritual.

Although the Bible makes no mention of any prayers that accompanied the sacrifices, there was some liturgy, in the form of both blessings and petitions, that was recited during the Second-Temple period of sacrifices. For instance, after the incense was offered, the priests recited the Priestly Blessing (*Tamid* 7:2). The Shema prayer ("Hear O Israel . . .") and the Ten Commandments were recited daily by the priests. In addition, a special psalm for each day was chosen and recited by the Levites. (These psalms of the day continue to be recited daily in synagogues the world over.)

The members of the *Anshay Ma'amad* who were unable to travel to Jerusalem for the week gathered every day in a central place for prayer and Bible-reading. They held two daily prayer assemblies, one in the morning and the other in the afternoon, timed to coincide with the two daily communal sacrifices. An additional (*Musaf*) gathering at noon and a *Neilah* ("closing of the gates") prayer assembly at day's end were also held. The prayer gatherings themselves were called *ma'amadot* (from the Hebrew for "stands" or "posts").

Long after the Second Temple was destroyed and the system of watch posts abandoned, pious worshippers would remain after synagogue services to read portions of Genesis that were once part of the original Temple reading. Even today, certain prayerbooks have retained a section called *Ma'amadot*, which preserves the verses once read during Temple times.

The destruction of the Second Temple by the Romans in 70 c.e. effectively ended sacrifices as a form of Jewish worship. The rabbis, led by Yochanan ben Zakkai, ruled that study, prayer, and the performance of good deeds were acceptable substitutes for sacrifices. The Hebrew term *avodah,* which referred to the service in the Jerusalem Temple, was reinterpreted in Tractate *Taanit* 2a to refer to "the service of the heart"—prayer.

PRAYER IN THE BIBLE

Although sacrifices were the primary mode of communication with God in the Bible, prayer also appears as a form of communication between God and human beings. The concept of prayer in the Bible is based on the assumption that God exists, listens to prayers, and, at times, answers them. In general, biblical prayer consists of personal spontaneous pleas to God, since fixed liturgy did not exist during these times. Although no particular gestures in connection with prayer are mandated in the Bible, certain postures developed naturally to add emphasis to the prayer content: kneeling (Daniel 6:11), prostration (Joshua 7:6), bowing one's head (Genesis 24:26), lifting one's hands (1 Kings 8:22), and so forth. Often prayer was accompanied by fasting, mourning, and weeping, but the ultimate criterion remained sincerity of the heart (Isaiah 58:2–5). Later, biblical prayer gave rise to liturgical patterns, prayer formulas, and musical renderings, which will be discussed in a later chapter of this book.

Because the needs of people in biblical times were so numerous and complex, prayer often came to reflect a variety of human moods, hopes, fears, feelings, and desires. Biblical prayer takes on a variety of forms, including petition, confession, meditation, thanksgiving, praise, and intercession.

What follows is a partial listing of the earliest recorded prayers in the Bible. Each prayer will be listed in the following order:

Prayer: The words of the prayer and the prayer's biblical source.

Object: The goal or object of the prayer.

Speaker: The person who stated the prayer.

Outcome: The outcome of the prayer.

1. Prayer: And Abraham drew near and said: "Will You sweep away the righteous with the wicked? Peradventure there are fifty righteous within the city, will You indeed sweep away and not forgive the place for the fifty righteous that are therein?" (Genesis 18:23–24).

   Object: Abraham petitions God to forgive the sin of the Sodomites for the sake of righteous people.

   Speaker: Abraham.

   Outcome: God agrees that He will forgive the sin if ten righteous souls are found.

2. Prayer: And he said: "O Lord, the God of my master Abraham, send me, I pray You, good speed this day,

and show kindness to my master Abraham" (Genesis 24:12).

Object: Eliezer petitions God to help in the search for a suitable wife for Abraham's son Isaac.

Speaker: Eliezer, Abraham's trustworthy servant.

Outcome: Eliezer finds Rebekkah, whom Isaac marries.

3. Prayer: Isaac entreated the Lord for his wife, because she was barren (Genesis 25:21).

Object: Isaac petitions God to let his barren wife Rebekkah be able to bear children.

Speaker: Isaac.

Outcome: Rebekkah gives birth to twin sons, Jacob and Esau.

4. Prayer: And Jacob vowed a vow, saying: "If God be with me, and will keep me in this way that I go, and will give me bread to eat and raiment to put on, so that I come back to my father's house in peace, then shall the Lord be my God" (Genesis 28:20–21).

Object: This conditional vow asks God for prosperity in return for devotion to God.

Speaker: Jacob.

Outcome: No immediate outcome occurs, but Jacob ultimately becomes Israel, the third Patriarch of the Israelites.

5. Prayer: And Jacob said: "O God of my father Abraham, and God of my father Isaac, O Lord, who said to me:

'Return to your country, and to your kindred, and I will do you good.' I am not worthy of all the mercies and of all the truth that You have shown your servant. For with my staff I passed over this Jordan, and now I am become two camps. Deliver me, I pray You, from the hand of my brother, from the hand of Esau . . ." (Genesis 32:10–11).

Object: Jacob petitions God to protect him from Esau.

Speaker: Jacob, Esau's brother.

Outcome: Jacob and Esau reconcile, and Esau forgives Jacob.

6. Prayer: And he said: "O Lord, send, I pray You, by the hand of him whom You will send" (Exodus 4:13).

Object: Discouraged by his mission, Moses petitions God to choose an alternate leader.

Speaker: Moses.

Outcome: God becomes angry at Moses's reluctance to accept his charge.

7. Prayer: Who is like you, O Lord, among the mighty? Who is like You, glorious in holiness, revered in praises, doing wonders? (Exodus 15:11).

Object: Moses and the children of Israel sing this praise of God after being liberated from Egypt and crossing the Red Sea.

Speaker: Moses and the Israelites.

Outcome: As a result of the miracle of the splitting of the Red Sea, the Israelites are saved, and they sing a song to God.

8. Prayer: And Moses cried to the Lord, saying: "What shall I do to this people? They are almost ready to stone me" (Exodus 17:4).

   Object: The Israelites grow angry in the desert because of their lack of water, and blame Moses for their predicament.

   Speaker: Moses.

   Outcome: God hears the plea of Moses, and tells him to strike a rock with his rod. Moses does so, and water comes forth so that the people are able to quench their thirst.

9. Prayer: Moses returned to the Lord and said, "This people have sinned a great sin, and have made for themselves a god of gold. Yet now, if You will forgive their sin; if not, blot me, I pray You, out of Your book which You have written" (Exodus 32:31–32).

   Object: Moses entreats God to forgive the Israelites for their sin of constructing a golden calf.

   Speaker: Moses.

   Outcome: God will not permit Moses to suffer vicariously for the sins of his people. God then punishes the Israelites.

10. Prayer: I pray You, if I have found grace in Your sight, show me now Your ways, so that I may know You, to the end that I may find grace in Your sight . . . (Exodus 33:13).

    Object: Moses entreats God to reveal His attributes to him.

Speaker: Moses.

Outcome: God reveals the thirteen Divine attributes.

11. Prayer: The Lord bless you and keep you. The Lord make His face to shine on you and be gracious to you. The Lord lift up His countenance to you and give you peace (Numbers 6:24–26).

    Object: This is a formula for a blessing to the Israelite people.

    Speaker: God speaks to Moses.

    Outcome: This blessing becomes the official Priestly Blessing with which the priests bless the people of Israel. It continues to be used in modern times when parents bless their children on Friday evening.

12. Prayer: Moses cried to the Lord, saying: "Heal her now, God, I beseech you" (Numbers 12:13).

    Object: Moses cries to God to heal his sister Miriam, who has been struck with the dreaded disease of leprosy.

    Speaker: Moses.

    Outcome: Miriam is cured after seven days.

13. Prayer: And now, I pray You, let the power of the Lord be great, according as You have spoken, saying: The Lord is slow to anger and abounding in lovingkindness. . . . Pardon, I pray You, the sin of this people according to the greatness of Your lovingkindness, and according as You have forgiven this people, from Egypt even until now (Numbers 14:17–19).

Object: Moses petitions God to forgive the Israelites for believing the spies who presented the negative report of the Promised Land.

Speaker: Moses.

Outcome: God pardons the people of Israel.

14. Prayer: And I besought the Lord at that time, saying: "O Lord God, You have begun to show your servant Your greatness, and Your strong hand. For what god is there in heaven or on earth, that can do according to Your works, and according to Your mighty acts? Let me go over, I pray You, and see the good land that is beyond the Jordan . . ." (Deuteronomy 3:23–25).

Object: Moses prays to God to let him see and enter the Promised Land.

Speaker: Moses.

Outcome: God tells Moses to cease petitioning Him about this matter. Moses ultimately sees the Promised Land from the banks of the Jordan River, but he is not permitted to enter it.

15. Prayer: The Rock, His work is perfect, for all His ways are justice. A God of faithfulness and without sin, just and right is He . . . (Deuteronomy 32:4).

Object: Moses ends his life of service to God and the children of Israel with a hymn of joy in which he praises God for His dependability and justice.

Speaker: Moses.

Outcome: Moses is told that he will be allowed to see the Promised Land from a distance.

16. Prayer: And she vowed a vow, and said: "O Lord of hosts, if You will look upon the suffering of Your maidservant and will remember me, and not forget Your maidservant, but will grant Your maidservant a male child, then I will dedicate him to the Lord all the days of his life . . ." (1 Samuel 1:11).

Object: The barren Hannah petitions God to allow her to give birth to a son, whom she vows will be dedicated and totally devoted to God's service.

Speaker: Hannah.

Outcome: Hannah gives birth to Samuel.

17. Prayer: And Solomon stood before the altar of the Lord in the presence of the whole community of Israel, and spread the palms of his hands toward heaven; and he said: "O Lord, the God of Israel, in the heavens above or on the earth below there is no God like You, who keeps Your gracious covenant with Your servants, that walk before You in wholehearted devotion" (1 Kings 8:22–23).

Object: Solomon entreats God to bring His Presence to earth, focused in the Jerusalem Temple.

Speaker: Solomon.

Outcome: God causes His presence to dwell in the Temple.

18. Prayer: And when it was time to present the evening offering, the prophet Elijah came forward, and said: "O Lord, the God of Abraham, of Isaac, and of Israel, let it be known today that You are God in Israel and that I am Your servant, and that I have done all these things at Your request. Answer me, O Lord, answer

me, that this people may know that You, O Lord, are God . . ." (1 Kings 18:36–37).

Object: Elijah entreats God to destroy the pagan god Baal.

Speaker: The prophet Elijah.

Outcome: Fire from God descends and consumes Elijah's burnt offering, thus proving to the people that there is only one God in the world.

19. Prayer: Jonah prayed to the Lord from the belly of the fish. He said, "In my trouble I called to the Lord and He answered me" (Jonah 2:2–3).

Object: Jonah, having been swallowed by the big fish, prays to God for deliverance.

Speaker: Jonah.

Outcome: God hears Jonah's prayer and commands the fish to spew Jonah forth onto dry land.

20. Prayer: I prayed to the Lord my God, making confession, thus: "O Lord, the great and awesome God, who keeps His covenant and mercy with those who love You and keep Your commandments. We have sinned, we have gone astray. . . . The shame, O Lord, is on us . . . because we have sinned against You. To the Lord our God belong mercy and forgiveness, for we have rebelled against Him" (Daniel 9:4–9).

Object: Daniel asks that God rebuild Jerusalem.

Speaker: The prophet Daniel.

Outcome: Jerusalem is rebuilt in seventy weeks.

PRAYER IN RABBINIC THOUGHT

It is typical of the Jewish approach that prayer, instead of being left up to the mood of the individual, is regulated. A variety of laws and customs govern prayer. There is no single viewpoint in rabbinic thought regarding prayer; rather, over the centuries, a variety of opinions have been presented, many of which have had broad consensus.

The primary biblical verse from which the rabbinic obligation to pray is derived is as follows (Deuteronomy 11:13): "You shall love the Lord your God, with all your heart, with all your soul, and with all your might." Rabbinic thinkers concluded (*Taanit* 2a) that this verse refers to prayer, because prayer is the means by which a person serves God with his or her heart. Thus, prayer is understood to mean "service of one's heart to God."

Of all the talmudic tractates, *Berachot* (literally, blessings) is the most informative source regarding the many laws and customs related to prayer and the worshipper. Here is a cross-section of rabbinic opinions about prayer that appear in *Berachot* and other rabbinic books.

THREE DAILY PRAYER SERVICES

Today, Jewish law mandates three daily prayer services in which traditional Jews are obliged to participate. These three services have been linked to the three Patriarchs, Abraham, Isaac, and Jacob. According to Rabbi Jose the son of Rabbi Chanina (*Berachot* 26b), prayer, in the form of the three daily services, was instituted by the Patriarchs themselves. Abraham is said to have instituted the morning service (*Shacharit*), based on the biblical verse (Genesis 19:27): "Abraham got up early in the morning where he had stood" ("stood" was interpreted to mean "prayed"). Isaac is said to have instituted the afternoon service (*Mincha*), based on the verse (Genesis 26:63): "Isaac went out to meditate in the field at eventide" ("meditate" was understood to mean "pray"). Finally, Jacob was said to have instituted the evening prayer service, as it is written (Genesis 28:11): "And he lighted upon the place" ("lighted" was interpreted to mean "prayed").

COMMUNAL PRAYER

According to most rabbinic opinion, communal prayer is of greater significance than private prayer. Though an individual is permitted to pray alone if unable to participate with a *minyan* (i.e., quorum of ten), the preferred situation has always been group prayer. Maimonides, the twelfth-century Jewish philosopher and law codifier, stressed the importance of communal prayer in the following paragraph from his *Laws of Prayer* (8:1):

> Prayer of the congregation is always heard by God. Even if there are sinners among them, the Holy One, blessed be He, does not reject the prayer of the congregation. Therefore, a person should always associate himself with the congregation, and not recite his prayers by himself any time he is able to pray with the congregation. . . . Whoever has a synagogue in his town and does not worship there with the congregation is called a bad neighbor.

People need each other's support in times of joy and sorrow. The following talmudic statement from *Berachot* 29b–30a demonstrates the importance of associating with a congregation of people:

> Rabbi Jacob said in Rav Chisda's name: Whoever goes on a journey must recite the prayer for the journey. What is it? "May it be Your will, O Lord my God, to lead me in safety and direct my steps in safety. . . . Praised are You, God, who listens to prayer." Abaye said: "One should always associate with the congregation." How should one then recite the prayer for traveling? "May it be Your Will, O Lord our God, to lead *us* in safety and direct *our* steps in safety. . . ."

NOT PROLONGING THE PRAYER EXPERIENCE

Too much reflection on one's prayer in the expectation that it will be answered is discouraged. In tractate *Shabbat* 10a we learn that Rabbi Hamnuna was rebuked

for prolonging his prayer and not occupying himself
more with study.

PROPER CONCENTRATION

Jewish law has always required the worshipper to be
aware that it is God who is being addressed, to "know
before Whom you are standing" (*Berachot* 28b). The
original Chassidim used to prepare for an hour and then
pray, in order to direct their minds to God (*Berachot*
5:1).

To transform reading from a prayerbook into sincere
prayer, one must have proper intent and direct one's mind
to God. The Hebrew word for such intent is *kavanah*. The
Talmud teaches that "the person who prays must direct his
heart to heaven" (*Berachot* 31a). The importance of the
worshipper's mood is reiterated in the talmudic dictum,
"One stands up to pray only when in a respectful frame of
mind" (*Berachot* 5:1).

The danger inherent in regulated prayer is the possibility
of turning one's prayer experience into a rote and mechanical routine. Rabbi Eliezer noted this pitfall centuries
ago when he stated: "One who makes his prayer a fixed
task, that prayer is not [true] supplication" (*Berachot* 4:4).
One way of avoiding the problem of fixed routine in prayer
was to recite a new prayer each day. This advice was
offered in the Jerusalem Talmud (*Berachot* 4:4).

Maimonides, the medieval philosopher, encouraged
people to add their own special prayers of need in the
prayer known as the *Amidah*: "If someone wants to add
to each of the intermediate blessings, he may do so.
How? If he is concerned about someone sick, he seeks

compassion for him in the blessing for the sick, according to his own eloquence . . ." (*Laws of Prayer* 6:2–3).

In the synagogue, a prayer service that includes a great deal of talking indicates an obvious lack of *kavanah* and proper spirit. Those guilty of idle chatter have been condemned as sinners in the *Code of Jewish Law* (Orach Chayyim 124:7).

Finally, should circumstances make it necessary for a worshipper to choose between saying more prayers without proper intention and saying fewer of them with the right intention, rabbinic teaching has always favored the choice of fewer prayers with proper intention (*Code of Jewish Law*, Orach Chayyim 1:4).

HEBREW, THE PREFERRED LANGUAGE OF PRAYER

Hebrew is called the "holy tongue" in rabbinic thought. It is the language of the prophets, the language of the Bible, and the language of the modern state of Israel. According to rabbinic opinion, Hebrew is the preferred language for prayer. It is not essential for prayers to be said in Hebrew, however, for Jewish law (*Code of Jewish Law*, Orach Chayyim, 101:4) rules that a person may pray in any language he or she understands. In fact, in talmudic times the rabbis decreed that some prayers, including Kaddish, be said in Aramaic, the commonly spoken language of the day, because so many people did not understand Hebrew.

Today there are many Jewish worshippers who do not know Hebrew and are unable to pray in the holy tongue. It is permissible, therefore, for such individuals to pray in the language they understand. Many congregations today offer Hebrew reading classes, for most congregations prefer to pray collectively in Hebrew, the sacred tongue to countless generations of Jews in both Israel and the Diaspora.

PROPER FORMS OF PRAYER

Not every prayer is a valid one, according to rabbinic opinion. For instance, if a person prays to God to change the past, that is called a prayer in vain (in Hebrew, *tefillah lashav*). The example given in the Talmud (*Berachot* 9:3) is that of a man, whose wife is already pregnant, who prays: "May it be God's will that my wife bears a boy."

According to the talmudic tractate *Baba Kamma* (92a), if a person needs something for himself but prays to God to grant that very thing to his neighbor who needs it, such an unselfish prayer causes God to grant him his wish first. It has always been considered meritorious for people to include others in their prayers.

ADDRESSING PRAYERS DIRECTLY TO GOD

Angels in the Hebrew Bible are messengers who carry out divine commands and promises. Even with the proliferation of angels in the liturgy, prayers are not to be addressed to angels, according to rabbinic opinion. In the Jerusalem Talmud (*Berachot* 9:1), we are told: "God says, 'When a person is in trouble do not cry out to the angel Michael or to the angel Gabriel, but to Me and I will answer immediately.'" The sincere worshipper is offered a "direct line," so to speak, to God, and must not rely and turn to intermediaries such as angels or the departed souls of loved ones for prayer.

CORRECT POSTURE DURING PRAYER

Standing has always been deemed a sign of respect. There are many times during the course of a Jewish worship service when standing is required as a mark of respect and to call attention to all especially important passage. The prayer par excellence for standing is the *Amidah* (which, literally, means "standing"). The correct posture for this prayer was established centuries ago. It can be summarized by the following passage of Maimonides (*Laws of Prayer* 5:4):

> What is the correct posture? When someone is standing and reciting the *Amidah*, his feet should be close together [i.e., at attention]. He should cast his eyes down, as if looking at the ground, and direct his thoughts upward, as if standing in heaven. He rests his hand on his heart, right over left. He should stand like a servant before his master, in terror, awe, and fear, and not rest his hands on his hips.

BODY AND SOUL

Cleanliness and care of one's body and soul is critical to a dignified and proper prayer experience. Washing and grooming before prayer is essential. Here are three sources of early-morning preparation for prayer:

1. It is forbidden for one to eat anything or do any work after daybreak until one prays the Morning Service (Maimonides, *Laws of Prayer* 6:4).

2. One who is thirsty or hungry is considered like a sick person. If a person is able to be attentive, then that

person should pray. If not, and if one desires, one need not pray until one has had something to drink (*Code of Jewish Law*, Orach Chayyim 89:4).

3. One does not stand praying the *Amidah* wearing a money belt, or with head uncovered, or barefoot (Maimonides, *Code of Jewish Laws of Prayer* 5:5).

Prayer in Medieval Thought, Kabbalah, and Chassidism

MEDIEVAL THINKERS AND PRAYER

Medieval Jewish thinkers had relatively little discussion about the intellectual difficulties inherent in the worship experience. Perhaps the greatest medieval philosopher and thinker, Maimonides, cautioned that it is beyond the capacity of the human mind to comprehend the totality of God, and formulated his so-called "doctrine of attributes." According to Maimonides, nothing positive can be said of God, because God is a simple being, and any positive attribute, such as "powerful" or "eternal," would imply that these qualities were "added" to the simple nature of God, making God a composite being. Therefore, the only real attributes of God are the negative ones. Thus, when we state that "God is one," we mean that "God is not many" and that He has no equal. In Maimonides's standard liturgy, he permitted the use of only those divine attributes in prayer that were ordained by the prophets, and he was opposed to the unsystematic writing of hymns. He held that it is a biblical duty for the Jew to pray daily with adequate concentration, which means emptying the mind of all other thoughts.

Joseph Albo, the fifteenth-century Spanish philosopher, attempted to answer the theological question concerning why a person needs to pray to God if God is omniscient and already knows the needs and desires of all human beings. In his *Book of Principles* (4:18), he wrote that God's assistance is dependent upon many different forms of human effort, including that of prayer.

Bachya ibn Pakuda, one of the best-known medieval Jewish moral philosophers, wrote a book titled *Chovot ha-Levavot (Duties of the Hearts)*. In the third chapter, he discussed divine worship, which is the expression of a person's gratitude to God. In order to fulfill his duties to God, ibn Pakuda advocated a number of virtues, among them the fact that a person's intentions must coincide with his actions in aiming toward the service of God. "Prayer without concentration," he stated, "is like a body without a soul" (*Chovot ha-Levavot* 8:3). He defined the genuine ascetic as a person who directs all of his actions to the service of God, while at the same time fulfilling his functions within society. The highest form of spiritual life is the love of God.

Joseph ibn Tzaddik of Cordova wrote *Sefer ha-Olam haKatan (The Book of Microcosm)*. For ibn Tzaddik, the attributes of actions are important for providing models for human conduct. For example, just as God is good and merciful, so too should people be good and merciful. Thus, to follow God's ways means to emulate God's attributes.

KABBALAH AND PRAYER

Mystics have often striven to achieve communion with God through meditation, prayer, and fasting. They yearn for their souls to rise heavenward and unite with God. Perhaps the best-known mystical statement on prayer is found in the *Book of Mysticism*—the basic kabbalistic text called the *Zohar* (meaning "splendor")—on the wondrous dream of Jacob's ladder, whose base stood on the ground and whose top reached to the heavens. This ladder, says the *Zohar*, is prayer.

Judaism has a long tradition of mysticism, known from the fourteenth century on as Kabbalah. One of the most famous kabbalists was the sixteenth-century Isaac Luria, known as the Ari. His branch of Kabbalah, called "Lurianic," holds that people can attain union with the Divine Spirit through intense concentration. According to Luria, a person who performs a religious obligation (*mitzvah*) is contributing to the mending of the universe itself. Prayer plays an important part in this process of mending (*tikkun*, in Hebrew). Each *mitzvah* is to be accompanied by the recitation of a formula declaring that the act was done for the purpose of "uniting the Holy One, praised be He, and His *Shechinah*, out of fear and love." Prayer is, thus, a vehicle by which a person's soul ascends to God.

Through prayer, one can also influence the upper spheres of the universe, where God dwells. The *Zohar* states: "Whoever prays with tears before the Almighty can procure the cancellation of any chastisement that has been decreed against him" (1 *Zohar* 223a).

In order to do this, one needs to be able to concentrate fully on the act of prayer. Thus, the true worshipper, with proper *kavanah*, can change the spiritual world of the universe and bring a person into an intimate relationship with God.

Kabbalists, in general, have always remarked on the difficulty of petitionary prayer to God, who is unchanging. Their view is that prayer cannot be offered to God as He is in Himself, but only to God as He is manifested in the ten divine spheres or luminaries through which God is revealed. Thus, for example, God is not directly entreated to show mercy: rather, prayer is directed to God as He is manifested in the divine sphere or attribute of lovingkindness.

Kabbalists substituted for the older doctrine of *kavanah* the concept of special intentions, known as *kavanot*. These so-called meditations on the realm of the divine spheres require mystics to concentrate on the actual realm of divine potencies and to direct their minds to the supernal mysteries that govern them, rather than to simply concentrate on the plain meaning of the various prayers.

In many mystical writings there is a connection between communion with God (in Hebrew, *devaykut*) and prophecy, which is the outcome of such union between human being and God. Moses, the greatest of all the prophets, was described as a man who was able to achieve a lasting state of *devaykut*. When this state of communion is realized, the Holy Spirit comes into contact with the mystic and gives him wondrous spiritual abilities.

PRAYER IN CHASSIDISM

Modern Chassidism, as a religious and social movement, springs from the teachings of the eighteenth-century Rabbi Israel Baal Shem Tov. The Baal Shem Tov taught that all people are equal before God—the ignorant as well as the learned—and that prayerful devotion and humility are more acceptable in heaven than intellectual attainments. He often sought communion with God in the woods and the fields, emphasizing that life itself is a divine manifestation.

One of the Baal Shem Tov's principal teachings was that every *mitzvah*, including that of daily worship, must be done with great enthusiasm; a mere mechanical and lifeless performance is of little value. For the Chassid, prayer is frequently seen as one of the most important religious activities.

Chassidism incorporates a great deal of body movement into prayer. Vigorous swaying (known as "shuckling"), laughter, dancing, and the singing of *niggunim* (melodies without words) have been employed by the Chassidim in order to attain a state of ecstasy and self-forgetfulness during prayer.

THE LANGUAGE OF PRAYER

PRAYER AS HEBREW POETRY

The language of Jewish prayer is Hebrew. Although it is permissible to pray in any language, Hebrew has always been the preferred language for a variety of reasons. It is the language of the Bible, and the Holy Tongue of the Jewish people. Praying in Hebrew thus ties the Jews to their ancient heritage. Hebrew is also the official language of the modern state of Israel, and praying in Hebrew helps to forge the important bond between Jews and their homeland.

Prayers, for the most part, are poems, often written by persons who had a wondrous experience that they attempted to capture in words. The words of poetry are allusive, as compared to words of prose, which are much more denotative. That is to say, whereas prose tends to direct specific meanings to its ideas, prayer as poetry tends to gently suggest a variety of meanings in its words. The prayer writers often chose symbols and metaphors to express their true feelings. In this way, the words of the prayerbook mean different things to different people and continue to evoke new impressions and ideas in the minds of the worshippers.

FIXED VERSUS SPONTANEOUS PRAYER

One of the great debates in rabbinic times, as well as in our own, has been whether prayers ought to be fixed in a specific order or whether it is more advantageous for worshippers to create their own original prayers each time they wish to pray. The question, in a nutshell, is: Which is better, fixed or spontaneous prayer? The debate continues today. Although the norm is clearly to pray in a structured setting (i.e., synagogue) using a fixed order of prayers in a prayerbook, the rabbis gave ample opportunity for personal prayer and meditation. Today, there are prayer groups that continue to use this rabbinic dispensation by writing and creating new and original prayers that they use in a less structured setting in their own group settings.

Twenty centuries ago, rabbinic scholars discussed the need for a fixed and detailed order to liturgy. Here are several incidents recorded in the Talmud that relate to the importance of the fixed, structured prayer system:

1. They entered a town and found a cantor who recited, "The great, powerful, awesome, mighty, dauntless God," and they silenced him. They said, "You are not allowed to add to the phrasing that the rabbis have

established for blessings" (Jerusalem Talmud, *Bera-chot* 9:112d).

2. Rabbi Yose says, "Whoever changes the phrasing that the sages determined for blessings has not fulfilled his obligation" . . . Rav said, "Any blessing that does not mention God's name is not a blessing" (*Berachot* 40b).

3. A person reading the Shema prayer in the evening is required to mention the Exodus from Egypt as part of the prayer *Emet v'Yatziv*. Rabbi Judah the Prince says, "One must mention God's kingship in it." Others say, "One must mention the parting of the Red Sea and the plague of the killing of the first-born sons." Rabbi Joshua ben Levi says, "One must mention them all, and must say, 'Rock of Israel and his Redeemer'" (Jerusalem Talmud, *Berachot* 1:3d).

Here are several citations related to the importance of enthusiasm and spontaneity in prayer:

1. Be careful when saying the Shema and *Amidah* prayers. When you do pray, do not make your prayer fixed, but rather compassionate and supplicatory before God (*Ethics of the Fathers* 2:18).

2. "Bless God." Resh Lakish said, "Whoever responds 'Amen' with all his strength, the gates of the Garden of Eden are opened up for him, as it is written, 'Open the gates and the righteous nation that keeps the faith will enter'" (*Shabbat* 119b).

3. A person who is praying must feel in his heart the meaning of the words on his lips, and consider that

God's presence is opposite him, and put aside all thoughts that distress him, until his thoughts and intentions are clear in his prayer. He must give consideration. If he were speaking to a sovereign, he would organize his words and give them proper attention so that he would not make errors. How much the more so before the Sovereign of sovereigns, the Holy One, blessed be He, who explores all thoughts (Chayyim, *Code of Jewish Law* 98).

4. If a person wants to add to each of the intermediate blessings [in the *Amidah*], he may do so. How? If he is concerned about someone who is ill, he seeks compassion for him in the blessing of the sick, according to his own effectiveness. . . . It is done in this way in every blessing (Maimonides, *Laws of Prayer* 6:2–3).

5. The three daily services may not be shortened, but a person may add to them. If a person wants to pray all day, he may do so. The prayers that he adds are like a free-will offering. Thus, one must make an appropriate thought as if it were new in each of the intermediate blessings [of the *Amidah*] (Maimonides, *Laws of Prayer* 1:9).

6. If a person prays only according to the exact fixed prayer and adds nothing from his own mind, his prayer is not considered proper (*Berachot* 28a).

7. Rabbi Abahu would add a new prayer to his worship every day. Rabbi Aha in the name of Rabbi Yose said: "It is necessary to add new words to the fixed prayers each time they are recited" (*Berachot* 4a).

8. Every word of your prayer should be like a rose that you pick from its bush. You continue to gather the roses until you have formed a bouquet and can offer it as a beautiful blessing to God (Bratzlaver Rebbe).

9. The Holy One, blessed be He, desires the heart (*Sanhedrin* 106b).

MUSIC AND PRAYER

Words do not constitute the only form of prayer in Judaism. Music's power to arouse the emotions has made it a factor in prayer since biblical times. The biblical verse, "Sing to God with thanksgiving, sing praises upon the harp to our God" (Psalms 147:7), points to an illustrious tradition of both vocal and instrumental song among the early Israelites. Psalm 150, known as the "musical psalm," describes the many instruments that were used during Temple times. Exodus records the exultant song of prayer that Moses and the Israelites sang after crossing the Red Sea.

The Talmud (*Arachin* 11a) considers song to be a way of serving God in joy and gladness. It is not surprising that, during Temple times, musical instruments were used to enhance worship. Although the use of instrumental music in services was banned as a sign of mourning after the destruction of the Second Temple, vocal music has remained an essential component of prayer and Bible reading, as can be evidenced by the chanting from the Torah.

The first written fragments of ancient synagogue melodies discovered by musiocologists date from the twelfth century. These fragments were found in the Cairo Genizah, a storeroom in the synagogue in Old Cairo. The melodies are said to be very similar to the church chants that were being sung at the time, but with Hebrew texts.

The Hebrew word *nusach* generally refers to the accepted way of chanting the prayer-service liturgy. It consists of a series of musical modes—groups of tones within a musical scale. In Jewish music, doing the *nusach* correctly is often more important than the correctness of the rhythm or harmony of the music. The ultimate purpose of the *nusach* is to convey the real meaning of the words that are chanted and listened to by the worshippers.

In addition to these musical motifs, many prayers have their own special melodies. Some of these tunes are called *mi-Seenai* ("from Sinai"), because it is difficult to ascertain their exact origin.

From this gigantic mass of general customs and musical influences, two distinct bodies of Jewish music and prayer have evolved over the centuries: the Ashkenazic (i.e., Jews of Western and Northern Europe and Russia) and the Sephardic (i.e., Jews from Greece, North Africa, and parts of the Middle East, originating in Spain).

THE CANTOR AND PRAYER

The cantor (*chazzan*, in Hebrew) is the leader of the congregational worship service. Acting as emissary of the congregation, the cantor leads the congregation in the chanting of prayers. Early in Jewish life, the emissary of the congregation was simply referred to as a *shaliach tzibbur*—representative of the congregation who was knowledgeable in the prayers and the melody lines. By the Middle Ages, the official profession of "cantor" arose and began to govern synagogue music. As a rule, the *chazzan* was a person of extensive learning and of high esteem. Consideration of character took precedence over voice quality, although a pleasant voice was certainly appreciated. Before the advent of printed prayerbooks, the cantor was the only member of the congregation who possessed a prayerbook manuscript. The congregation, therefore, was greatly dependent on the cantor, and was actually led by him, in the worship services.

The period from the end of the nineteenth century until World War II has been described as the Golden Era of *Chazzanut*. The best cantorial music of some of the most outstanding cantors drew many to attend worship services.

Choral music and choirs date back to the time of the First Temple. It was following an instrumental overture with a chorus that King Solomon rendered his prayer of dedication upon the completion of the First Temple. Singing in the Temple basically remained the privilege of the Levites, who served in the capacity of Temple choir. The modern synagogue choir owes its origin to the spirit of the Italian Renaissance. Leone Modena founded the first artistic choir in synagogue history at the beginning of the seventeenth century. Today, choirs have become an integral part of many synagogues among the various streams of Judaism throughout the world.

BODY LANGUAGE AND PRAYER

Deuteronomy (6:5) states that one should love God with all one's soul, heart, and might. Jews have developed their own set of rules and customs related to how the body is to be used during a prayer experience. Sitting, standing, bending, bowing, and kissing are just a few of the many liturgical body-language actions. These customs, rules, and regulations were intended to enhance the prayer experience and to help bring the words of the liturgy to life. The following is a summary of the major body-language motions (listed by category) that are used during a typical worship service.

Standing

Standing has always been considered a sign of respect. For example, one always stands for the singing of the national anthem. Similarly, there are many times during the course of a prayer service when standing is an appropriate way to honor God as the Sovereign of Sovereigns.

The prayer par excellence for standing is the *Amidah* (which means "standing"). It is customary during this prayer to stand erect, with heels together, as a sign of reverence. Some of the other prayers for which Jews customarily stand include the Morning Blessings, *Baruch She'amar*, Psalm 136, Psalm 129, the Song of Moses, *Yishtabach*, Kaddish, *Aleynu, Hallel*, Psalms of Praise, and any time the Holy Ark is open.

Bowing

In early Jewish history it was customary for Jewish worshippers to prostrate themselves to the ground as a sign of reverence for God. In modern times, this is done only during a portion of the High Holy Day services.

Bowing is a sign of humility, and it is customary to bow a number of times during the prayer service. There are four places for bowing during the *Amidah* prayer: at the beginning and the end of the first blessing (i.e., "ancestors"), and at the beginning and the end of the eighteenth blessing of the thanksgiving. It is also customary to bow from the waist on the word *barechu* in the prayer *Barechu*, which was the official call to worship during Temple times. At one point during *Aleynu, Va'anachnu korim umishtachavim umodim* ("We bend the knee, bow, and give thanks"), it is customary to bend the knees and then bow.

Rising on Tiptoes

During *Kedushah*, the Sanctification prayer, it is customary to rise three times onto one's toes, once for each mention of the word *kadosh* ("holy"). This act symbolizes a reach toward the heavens.

Approaching God

Immediately preceding the verse that opens the *Amidah, Adonai sifatai tiftach ufi yagid tehilatecha* ("My Lord, open my mouth so that I may praise You"), it is customary for the worshipper to retreat three steps and then advance three steps, to symbolize one's reverent approach of the Sovereign.

Taking Leave of God

During the words *Oseh shalom bimromav hu ya'aseh shalom aleynu ve'al kol Yisrael* ("May He who estab-

lishes peace in the heavens grant peace to Israel"), the
custom is as follows: Take three steps backward; at
shalom bimromav bend left at the waist; at *hu ya'aseh
shalom* bend right at the waist; at *aleynu ve'al kol Yisrael*
bend forward at the waist. Then, at *ve'imru* ("Now
respond"), stand erect. This is the reverse of the approach to God at the beginning of the *Amidah*. We then
complete our leave-taking of God at the end of the
Amidah prayer by taking three steps forward.

Closing the Eyes

During the recitation of the Shema ("Hear [O Israel]"),
the custom is to close one's eyes and cover them with the
hand. This prevents distraction, thus allowing the worshipper to concentrate on God's Oneness.

Kissing

Kissing is a sign of love and affection for God and God's
commandments. During the third paragraph of the Shema
(i.e., Numbers 15:37–41), the custom is to kiss the four
tzitzit (fringes) of one's prayer shawl (*tallit*) three times—
once each time the word *tzitzit* is mentioned. In this way,
one is thus symbolically embracing God's *mitzvot*.

The Torah is kissed when it is carried through the
synagogue. One does this by extending a hand to the
Torah mantle and then kissing the hand. Some people
touch the Torah with the edge of a prayerbook or prayer
shawl, and then kiss that. The Torah scroll is also kissed
before the blessing is recited over it. This is usually done
by taking the edge of the *tallit* (or the sash that is used to
tie the Torah), touching the outside of the scroll with it,
and then kissing the *tallit* or sash.

If one accidentally drops a prayerbook or Bible, the custom is to kiss it as a sign of respect.

Finally, an Ark curtain may be kissed before it is opened or after it is closed, when the Torah scroll is put away.

Swaying

The swaying motion (known as "shuckling") that many worshippers adopt during prayer is a way of involving one's entire heart and soul in the prayer experience. Some have explained the custom of rocking back and forth as symbolizing the verse in Psalms 35:10: "All my limbs shall declare, 'O Lord, who is like You.'" When one sways back and forth, it is as though one's entire body is caught up in the prayer experience. Shuckling is particularly noticeable among Orthodox Jews, especially the Chassidic sects.

SYNAGOGUE GEOGRAPHY

A BRIEF HISTORY

The synagogue, as a place of congregational prayer and public instruction, came into existence long before the destruction of the Second Temple and the cessation of sacrificial worship. It is generally assumed that the synagogue took shape during the Babylonian captivity in the sixth century B.C.E., when the Jews were separated from their Temple and its centralized sacrificial system, and that it was brought to Judea after the rebuilding of the Temple and the return to Zion. By the time of the Second Temple, many synagogues were already in existence.

Egypt is known to have had many synagogues during the third century B.C.E. One of its most famous ones was the celebrated synagogue of Alexandria, Egypt.

Throughout its illustrious history, the synagogue has

been the spiritual home of the Jewish people. It has a variety of names in Hebrew: "house of prayer" (*beit tefillah*), "house of study" (*beit midrash*), "house of assembly" (*beit knesset*), and "little sanctuary" (*beit mikdash me'at*). The Yiddish word for synagogue translates to "school" (*schul*). Not only has the synagogue been a place for worship, but it also has been a gathering place for study, *tzedakah*, and social work. In bygone years, travelers and strangers were fed there. It is likely that no human institution has had a longer continuous history than the synagogue.

SYNAGOGUE GEOGRAPHY

Detailed laws regulate the following aspects of the synagogue and its use: the design and location of the building, its furnishings and interior design, proscribed use of the synagogue's contents, and the ownership and disposal of the building.

Few specific situations relate to the general exterior. Synagogues are required to have windows, a requirement taken from a verse in Daniel 6:11 that describes how Daniel prayed by windows that faced the holy city of Jerusalem. According to the Talmud (*Berachot* 34b), windows allow the worshipper to see the sky, which is known to inspire reverence.

The requirement to build a dwelling for the Torah scrolls took the form of an enclosure known as the *aron hakodesh* (Holy Ark). The Ark was to be built in an elevated position, and, since the custom during prayer is to face East (i.e., in the direction of Jerusalem), arks were built on the eastern wall of a synagogue. Covering the ark is a *parochet* (curtain), which takes its name from its counterpart in the ancient Temple: the curtain that hung in front of the Holy of Holies. The curtain is often embroidered with pictures or biblical quotations.

The reader's desk, upon which the Torah scroll is placed, was traditionally located in front of the Ark. The Torah is read from the *bimah*, an elevated platform, which years ago was almost always located at the center of the synagogue so that the entire congregation could hear the reading. Today, in some modern synagogues, the *bimah* is located in the front of the synagogue, thus creating more seating space for its congregants.

A lamp is usually suspended in front of the Holy Ark. Called in Hebrew the *ner tamid* ("eternal light"), it consisted in centuries past of a wick burning in olive oil. Today, in most synagogues, it is an electric lamp that burns twenty-four hours a day. The eternal light is a symbolic reminder of the *menorah*, the ancient seven-branched candelabrum that burned in the Temple. Originally, the *menorah* was placed in a niche in the western wall of the synagogue in remembrance of the position of the *menorah* in the Temple. Later, it was suspended in front of the Holy Ark. The eternal light is seen as a symbol of God's eternal presence and the eternal faith of the Jewish people.

In Orthodox synagogues, women have their own separate seating area, reminiscent of the special women's section in the Temple. The *mechitzah* is a type of partition or screen that serves to separate the men's seating section from the women's in the synagogue. In almost all Conservative, Reform, and Reconstructionist synagogues, the *mechitzah* has been abolished.

The *Code of Jewish Law* (Orach Chayyim 150:5)

specifies that the seating arrangement in the synagogue should provide for the elders to sit adjacent to the Ark and facing the congregation. This law is generally not followed today, since the ruling was considered applicable only at a time when synagogue seats were allocated by the community.

OBJECTS THAT DECORATE THE TORAH SCROLL

A number of objects may decorate and enhance a Torah scroll.

Rimmonim: Decorative finials, usually made of silver but sometimes made of wood, adorn the top of the Torah rollers.

Choshen: A silver breastplate or shield that decorates and protects the front of the Torah. It is reminiscent of the breastplate worn by the High Priest during Temple times.

Yad: A metal or wooden pointer used by the reader to help keep the place when reading from the Torah scroll.

Keter: A silver crown that often adorns the top of a Torah scroll.

Avnet or *wimpel*: The belt that is wrapped around the two sides of the Torah scroll.

Atzai chayyim: Literally "trees of life," this refers to the wooden Torah handles around which the parchment is rolled.

Mantle: This is the decorative cover that is slipped over the parchment and Torah handles.

THE ETHICAL DIMENSION OF
SYNAGOGUE PRAYER SERVICES

The ancient rabbis were the first to set a personal example in the daily giving of *tzedakah*. The Talmud (*Baba Batra* 10a) describes Rabbi Elazar, who would always give a coin to a poor person before praying. Maimonides, in *The Laws of the Poor*, tells of the many famous sages who always performed acts of charity before saying their prayers.

Many synagogues have a charity box (known as a *pushke*) that is used for money collection during daily services (except for the Sabbath and holy days) and is kept in a small chapel. This act of righteous giving assists the worshipper in remembering that all prayer ought to be seen as a way of helping people in need.

SYNAGOGUE FUNCTIONARIES

Rabbi: The word *rabbi* means "my teacher." Accordingly, the rabbi gives sermons, explains the service, often announces the pages, and recites blessings during services. Aside from these functions in the synagogue service itself, the rabbi also acts as teacher, counselor, leader, and so forth.

Cantor: Also called the *chazzan*, the cantor chants and sings the prayers. The cantor may also read the Torah, teach the bar and bat mitzvah students, and act as spiritual leader and counselor like the rabbi.

Gabbai or *shammash*: The *gabbai* or *shammash* is the

coordinator of activities during the worship service. The gabbai may give out honors (i.e., *aliyot*), assist the Torah reader, and the like.

Torah reader: The Torah reader reads from the Torah on the Sabbath and Jewish festivals, and on Mondays and Thursday mornings. The Torah reader often is one of the abovementioned functionaries.

Ushers: Ushers often hand out the prayerbooks and Bibles to members of the congregation upon entering the synagogue sanctuary. They are also often responsible for Temple decorum.

Ba'al tefillah: This is a lay person, not a professional cantor, who is especially adept at leading the service. This person is religiously qualified to lead the prayers.

Shaliach tzibbur: This term means "emissary of the congregation." This is the person who actually leads the service. It may be the *chazzan*, the *ba'al tefillah*, or any other person called upon to fill the role.

PROSCRIBED USES OF A SYNAGOGUE AND ITS CONTENTS

A variety of laws relate to the behaviors that are proper and improper when in the synagogue. For instance, frivolity, gossiping, eating, drinking, beautifying oneself, sleeping, entering to escape inclement weather, transacting business, or using it as a shortcut to some other destination are all strictly forbidden activities. Dirt and rubbish are not permitted to collect in the synagogue.

When first entering a synagogue, one is required to clean one's shoes of mud. According to the Talmud (*Berachot* 6b), a person may run when going to synagogue, but when leaving must walk so as not to indicate a desire to get away from it.

All synagogue objects are considered sanctified, prayer-books and Bibles, the Holy Ark, the Ark curtain, and the like. When these are no longer usable, they must be stored or buried rather than destroyed.

If a congregation decides to split into two congregations, the holy objects are to be divided between the two congregations according to the size of their constituencies. If a synagogue is in a state of complete disrepair, it may not be demolished until another is provided to take its place. If a synagogue is in a state of possible collapse, it is then permitted to be demolished with the expectation that construction of a new one will begin immediately.

Prayer Garments

Many professions have dress codes or specialized uniforms that people wear while on the job. Uniforms are standards of dress that help to create the proper setting and feeling while a person is on the job.

Prayer also has a number of components to its uniform, including the *kipah* (head covering), the *tallit* (prayer shawl), *tefillin* (phylacteries), and the *kittel* (white robe), worn on Yom Kippur. In this chapter we will discuss the origin and nature of these ritual objects, which have become part of the prayer uniform of the worshipper.

KIPAH (SKULLCAP)

Throughout Jewish history, the attitude toward covering the head has varied. Drawings from the third century c.e.

depict Jews without hats. In the Middle Ages, many Jews wore hats during prayer and study only.

Centuries ago, the Talmud suggested that to cover one's head was a sign of respect and humility before God. In *Kiddushin* 31a we learn that Rav Huna would not walk four *amot* (i.e., six feet) without covering his head, for he said that the Divine Presence was above his head. The idea of covering one's head as a sign of awe and respect for God is also mentioned in *Kiddushin* 31a, and it was gradually endorsed by the Ashkenazic rabbis.

Although the Bible required Jewish priests (i.e., *kohanim)* to wear a special headdress much like a turban while officiating as a sign of respect and glory before God, the Torah makes no direct reference to the requirement for men and women to cover their heads.

The *yarmulke* or skullcap (*kipah*, in Hebrew) is the preferred headgear for many men today. The origin of the word is obscure, although it has been reasoned that *yarmulke* may be a shortened form of two Aramaic words, *yaray me-Elohecha* ("one who fears God"). The wearing of a skullcap is not mandated in either the Torah or the Talmud. Although the skullcap itself has no intrinsic holiness and no blessing is recited when putting it on, wearing it is considered a form of respect, especially while saying prayers. Orthodox Jewish men generally keep their heads covered both outside and inside the synagogue; Conservative, and most Reconstructionist, men cover their heads while praying in the synagogue (some may also choose to wear a headcovering outside the synagogue). In Reform congregations, covering one's head is optional.

In biblical times, women covered their heads with veils or scarves as a sign of modesty. In talmudic times,

too, women almost always covered their hair. Today,
most orthodox women cover their hair when they
appear in public both outside and inside the synagogue;
headcoverings vary from hats to kerchiefs to wigs. In
Reform, Conservative, and Reconstructionist congregations, covering the head is generally optional for women.

TALLIT (PRAYER SHAWL) AND *TZITZIT*

The *tallit*, or prayer shawl, can be traced back to biblical
times. The religious obligation to wear a *tallit* is found in
a biblical passage that became the third paragraph of the
Shema:

> Speak to the children of Israel and instruct them to make
> fringes for themselves on the corners of their garments
> throughout their generations. Let them attach a thread of
> blue to the fringe at each corner. That will be your fringe.
> Look at it and remember all of God's commandments
> and do them, so that you do not follow your heart and
> eyes in your sensual urge. Thus will you be reminded to
> observe all of My commandments and to be holy to your
> God (Numbers 15:37–40).

It is evident from this source that the fringes on the
corners of the garment were to be reminders of God's
commandments. In biblical days, there was no special
garment such as the prayer shawl of today. Rather, the
Israelites simply wore fringed garments as a form of
identification and a reminder that they were designated
to be a holy kingdom of priests.

During the period of the Second Temple, the design of
the fringe (*tzitzit*) and the garment itself became formal-

ized, with specific rules that described how they were to be fashioned and knotted.

Today, the *tallit* is traditionally worn by Jewish men, and by some women, at every morning service, Sabbath and weekdays (except on Tisha B'Av, the Fast of the Ninth of Av). It is also worn on the night of Yom Kippur, as a sign of additional sanctity. In some rites, the cantor wears a *tallit* during the afternoon and evening services.

The age of first donning a *tallit* differs in various communities. It is the custom among many traditional Ashkenazic Jews that only married men wear prayer shawls, though in some circles boys and single men wear them. The Sephardic custom is generally only for married men to wear them, although there are exceptions. For Reform Jews, the wearing of a *tallit* often is optional.

It is customary to bury Jewish men (and those women who wore a prayer shawl regularly in their lifetime) in the *tallit*. As an act of reverence for the dead, who are no longer able to perform the *mitzvot*, the *tzitzit* are removed from the *tallit* before the burial.

The fringes themselves are attached to two different types of garments. During the day, they are worn by traditional men under the shirt on a garment that has come to be known as *arba kanfot* (Hebrew for "four corners") or *tallit katan* (literally, "small *tallit*") This garment goes on over the head, much like a poncho. Since the biblical verse states that the fringes ought to be seen, some men let the fringes hang out so that they can be seen. The other kind of *tallit* is a fringed shawl that is worn over the shoulders like a cape.

Before the prayer shawl is put on, a blessing is said. This blessing often appears on the neckband, or *atarah*, of the *tallit*. Here is the blessing: "Blessed are You, Lord our God, Sovereign of the universe, Who has sanctified us with Your commandments and commanded us to wrap ourselves in the fringed garment."

Although women are not obligated to wear a *tallit* (the rabbis exempted them from time-related positive commandments), they may choose to do so. It is becoming more common for women in branches of Judaism other than Orthodoxy to choose to wear a *tallit*.

Many, although not all, strictly observant Jews pray with the *tallit* covering their head. This adds to their devotion and increases their power of concentration. During the prayer immediately preceding the Shema, the *tzitzit* are customarily gathered together and held around one's finger. This symbolizes the coming together of the four corners of the Earth. It is customary during the recitation of the last section of the Shema (Numbers 15:37–40), which deals with the commandment of the fringes, for the person wearing the prayer shawl to kiss them each of the three times that the word *tzitzit* (fringe) is mentioned. Some people kiss the *tzitzit* four times—once for each of the four letters of God's Name.

TEFILLIN (PHYLACTERIES)

One of the most distinguishing features of the weekday morning service is the wearing of *tefillin*. The English translation of this word is "phylacteries" (from the Greek word for "amulet"). *Tefillin* are two small black leather boxes containing tiny parchment scrolls inscribed with biblical passages, and bound by black leather straps.

There are four biblical sources for the commandment of wearing *tefillin*:

1. And it shall serve you as a sign on your arm and as a reminder on your forehead—in order that the Lord's teachings may be in your mouth—for with a mighty hand the Lord freed you from Egypt (Exodus 13:9).

2. And it shall be as a sign upon your arm, and as a symbol upon your forehead, that with a mighty hand the Lord freed us from Egypt (Exodus 13:16).

3. Bind them as a sign upon your arm and let them serve as a symbol upon your forehead (Deuteronomy 6:8).

4. Therefore impress these My words upon your very heart and upon your soul; bind them as a sign upon your arm and let them serve as a symbol upon your forehead (Deuteronomy 11:18).

Each of these four passages has as its theme the binding of one's body and one's mind to God. The four biblical passages are handwritten on parchment by a scribe and inserted in the boxes of both the arm *tefillin* and the head *tefillin*. In the arm *tefillin* they are written on one single piece of parchment, while in the head *tefillin* they are divided into four, each written on a separate piece of parchment, tied, and inserted into the box of the head *tefillin*. According to the biblical commentator Rashi, the passages appear, in both boxes, in the order of their occurrence in the Bible. According to his grandson Rabbi Tam, the passage from Deuteronomy 11:13–21, in both boxes, precedes that of Deuteronomy 6:4–9. Today, Rashi's order has been accepted as the traditional order of preference.

Tefillin are an ancient ritual, dating back well over two thousand years. Archaeologists have found sets of *tefillin* dating from the times of Bar Kochba, who led a revolution against the Romans in the year 132 c.e. These ancient *tefillin* are very similar to the ones that are worn today.

The following is a summary of *tefillin*, including their various component parts, the mode of wearing them, when to wear them, a rabbinic appraisal of their symbolism and importance, and some notable *tefillin* quotations.

The Components of *Tefillin*

1. *Tefillin shel rosh*: This is the head *tefillin*, consisting of four compartments holding each of the four pieces of sacred parchment with verses from Exodus and Deuteronomy.

2. *Tefillin shel yad*: This is the arm *tefillin*, containing one piece of parchment upon which is written all of the *tefillin* source verses from Exodus and Deuteronomy.

3. *Bayit*: Hebrew for "house," the *bayit* is the leather box that houses the parchment. The *bayit* of the head *tefillin* has four separate compartments into which the four pieces of parchment are placed. Unlike the *bayit* of the arm *tefillin*, the *bayit* of the head has a four-pronged Hebrew letter *shin* and a three-pronged letter *shin* etched on two sides. Some commentators have said that these letters are symbolic of the Three Patriarchs—Abraham, Isaac, and Jacob—and the four Matriarchs—Sarah, Rebekkah, Leah, and Rachel.

Others say that since the Hebrew numerical equivalent of the letter *shin* is 300, the letters serve as a reminder that *tefillin* are worn 300 out of the 354 days of the Jewish year. The unusual four-pronged *shin*, some have said, appeared on the tablet of the Ten Commandments. The commandments were engraved all the way through the tablets so that they could be read from either side. For a shin to be read both ways, it must be four-pronged so that there are three spaces in between.

4. *Retzuot*: These are the leather straps (singular, *retzuah*) that are used to tie the *batim* (plural of *bayit*) to the arm and head. The leather *retzuot* are made from the skin of kosher animals and are colored black on one side.

5. *Ma'abarta*: Extending from the back of the *bayit* is another piece of leather that forms a hollow extension. This is the *ma'abarta* (passageway) through which the leather strap is slipped in order to be able to tie the *bayit* to one's arm and head.

6. *Perudote*: These are the four separate compartments of the *bayit* that is part of the head *tefillin*.

7. *Teetura*: This is the square base of the *tefillin* upon which the *bayit* is situated.

8. *Kesher*: This refers to the knot on the leather straps of both the arm and the head *tefillin*. The knot allows the leather strap to be affixed to the arm as well as to the head. The knot on the head strap can be adjusted to fit.

9. *Giddin*: These are the threads that are used to sew the parchment into the *tefillin* boxes. The threads are

generally made from the hip muscles of kosher animals.

The Mode of Wearing *Tefillin*

The order of putting on the *tefillin*, which occurs after the *tallit* is put on (if one is worn), is carefully detailed in rabbinic law. The arm *tefillin* is put on first, placed on one's weaker upper arm, and the knot is tightened. A right-handed person always places the *bayit* opposite the heart, whereas a left-handed person puts it on the right arm. The strap is wound seven times around the arm between the elbow and the wrist, and the blessing "to put on the *tefillin*" is recited. The Ashkenazic custom is to wind the strap anticlockwise; the Sephardic custom is to wind it clockwise.

The head *tefillin* is then put on, as a second blessing on "the precept of *tefillin*" is pronounced.

The remaining part of the strap of the arm is then wrapped in a prescribed manner around the hand and the middle finger to form the Hebrew letters *shin* and *dalet*. There is a knot next to the *bayit* of the hand in the shape of the Hebrew letter *yud*. Together, these three Hebrew letters spell the word Shaddai—one of God's ancient names. While making the rings around the middle finger, symbolically representing one's betrothal to God, the worshipper recites the following from Hosea 2:21–22: "And I will betroth you to Me forever, I will betroth you in righteousness and in justice, in loving-kindness and in compassion. And I will betroth you to Me in faithfulness, and you shall know the Lord."

When to Wear *Tefillin*

Tefillin are worn on all weekdays, but not on the Sabbath or Festivals. The reason given in rabbinic thought is that the Torah refers to *tefillin* as a "sign" (*ot*, in Hebrew). The Sabbath itself is also called a sign, and the ancient Sages stated that no person requires more than one sign of God's covenant at any one time. The same rule was applied to Festivals. *Tefillin* are considered an adornment, and so are not worn the morning of Tisha B'av (Fast of the Ninth of Av), by the bereaved before a funeral, or the bridegroom on his wedding day. The official duty is put on *tefillin* begins when a young boy reaches the age of Jewish religious maturity (i.e., thirteen years and one day, according to his Hebrew birthday). It is usual in traditional Jewish circles for boys to begin to put on *tefillin* several weeks earlier, for practice.

Tefillin in Rabbinic Thought

The Talmud stresses the importance of wearing *tifillin* in a number of different ways. For example, in Tractate *Berachot* 6a, we are told that even God dons *tefillin*, hearing the verse, "Who is like Your people Israel, one people on Earth" (1 Chronicles 17:21). If *tefillin* are dropped accidentally, the rabbinic requirement is to fast for an entire day. The rabbis, in Tractate *Menachot* 43b, stated that "whosoever has *tefillin* on his head" is fortified against sinning.

Jewish mystics instituted a meditation before putting on *tefillin*. It includes the following: "God has commanded us to lay the *tefillin* upon the hand as a memorial of His outstretched arm; opposite the heart to indicate the duty of subjecting the longing and designs of our heart to God's service. And upon the head, over against the brain, thereby teaching that the mind, whose seat is in the brain, together with all senses and faculties, is to be subjected to God's service."

Classical *Tefillin* Quotations

Here are some quotations related to *tefillin* that appear in the Talmud, the Midrash, and mystical kabbalistic texts.

In the Talmud

1. *Tefillin* are Israel's strength. It is written (Deuteronomy 28:10): "And the peoples of the Earth shall see that God's name is called upon you, and they shall be awed by you" (*Berachot* 6a).

2. A person who washes his hands, puts on *tefillin*, says the Shema, and prays is considered to have built an altar and offered a sacrifice. That person is also said to have genuinely accepted upon himself the yoke of heaven (*Berachot* 14b).

3. Every single Jew is surrounded by seven *mitzvot*. He has *tefillin* on his arm and head, a *mezuzah* on his door, and four *tzitzit* on his garment. Thus, King David said (Psalms 119:164): "I will praise You each day with seven" (Tosefta, *Berachot* 6:31).

4. A person must constantly touch his *tefillin* and not take his mind from them (*Shabbat* 12a).

5. A person should be as dedicated in wearing *tefillin* as Elisha, the Master of Wings. Once the government

issued a decree that anyone wearing *tefillin* should be put to death. Elisha defied the decree and publicly wore *tefillin*. He was captured by one of the king's agents. They asked him, "What is in your hand?" Concealing his *tefillin*, he answered, "A dove's wing." When they forced open his hand, they found the wing of a dove in place of his *tefillin*. From then on, he was called Elisha, the Master of Wings (*Shabbat* 49a).

6. A person always needs a sign of his bond with God. The Sabbath is itself such a sign, but on weekdays, this sign is *tefillin* (*Eruvin* 96a).

7. One who does not wear *tefillin* is counted among those that are banned from God (*Pesachim* 113b).

8. *Tefillin* are called the glory of Israel (*Sukkah* 25a).

9. Who is a sinner with his body? The person who never wears *tefillin* (*Rosh Hashanah* 17a).

10. The students asked Rabbi Ada ben Ahavah, "Why were you worthy of such a long life?" He replied, "One reason is because I always wore *tefillin*" (*Taanit* 20b).

11. Abraham told the King of Sodom [Genesis 14:23], "I will not even take a thread or a shoe strap." Because of this, God gave Abraham's children the threads of *tzitzit* and the straps of *tefillin* (*Sotah* 44b).

12. God Himself showed Moses the knot of *tefillin* (*Menachot* 35b).

13. One who wears *tefillin* is worthy of long life (*Menachot* 35b).

In the Midrash

1. It was a time of religious persecution, and a person was being beaten to death. He said, "I defied their ban and risked my life to wear *tefillin*. Let me now die doing the will of my Father in heaven" (Leviticus Rabbah 32:1).

2. It is written [Psalms 91:7]: "A thousand shall fall at your side . . . it shall not come near you." Through the religious obligation of wearing *tifillin*, one is guarded from evil by a thousand angels (Numbers Rabbah 12:3).

3. It is written [Song of Songs 2:6]: "Let God's left hand be under my head, and God's right hand embrace me." God thus embraces a person who wears *tefillin* (Song of Songs Rabbah 2:17).

4. It is written [Song of Songs 8:6]: "Set Me for a seal on your heart, as a seal on your arm." The *tefillin* are this seal of God (Song of Songs Rabbah 8:4).

5. The Jewish people said to God, "We would like to immerse ourselves in the Torah day and night, but do not have the time." God answered, "Keep the *mitzvah* of *tefillin*, and I will count it as if you spent all of your time with My Torah" (Midrash Psalms 1).

6. The Messiah will come to give the world *mitzvot* such as *tefillin* (Midrash Psalms 1).

In Kabbalah

1. Happy is the person who wears *tefillin* and fathoms their mystery (1 *Zohar* 129a).

2. When a person wears *tefillin* and *tzitzit*, that person enters a realm where the Holy One surrounds him with the mystery of the highest faith (*Zohar* 140b).

3. The person who wears *tefillin* is crowned as on high. He enters the perfection of Unity and so resembles his Creator (*Zohar* 3:81a).

4. One who wears *tefillin* is called a king on earth, even as God is called a King in heaven (*Zohar* 3:169b).

5. A person is bound to the Mother of Israel with two signs, the *tefillin* and the covenant of Abraham (Tikkune *Zohar* 7a).

6. When a person wears *tefillin*, a voice proclaims to all the angels of the chariot who watch over prayer, "Give honor to the image of the King, the person who wears *tefillin*" (*Zohar* 55:124a).

7. When a person wakes up in the morning and binds himself with the holy mark of *tefillin*, four angels greet him as he leaves his door (*Zohar* Chadash 41b).

8. The straps of *tefillin* are like chains binding the Evil One (Tikkune *Zohar* Chadash 101b).

The Symbolism of *Tefillin*

A number of different symbols are involved in the religious obligation of donning *tefillin*. They include the following:

Binding oneself to God, both physically and spiritually.

A reminder of God's power in liberating the Jew from Egyptian bondage. Thus, wearing *tefillin* becomes a memorial for leaving the binding slavery of Pharaoh for the binding service of God.

A betrothal between the wearer of the *tefillin* and God. This is especially indicated by the convenantal theme of winding the strap around the fingers of the hand: "I will betroth you to Me forever. I will betroth you with righteousness, with justice, with love, and with compassion. I will betroth you to Me with faithfulness, and you shall love God" (Hosea 2:21–22).

KITTEL

The *kittel* is a white linen garment, often bound by a white belt, that is worn on a number of occasions, including the High Holy Days (Rosh Hashanah and Yom Kippur). It is worn by the leader of the Passover seder and by the groom at this wedding; it is also used as a burial shroud. The cantor wears it for the prayer for rain on Sukkot, the prayer for dew on Passover, and all Yizkor (memorial) services. The association of the color white with the concept of purity and solemn joy contributed to the special use of the *kittel* on all of these occasions.

THE BIRTH OF THE PRAYERBOOK

It is reasonably certain that, by the early days of the Second Temple, some form of group prayer existed among the Jewish people. During the next two or three hundred years, the prayer service—in addition to the Temple service—became an established mode of worship. That service likely included the recitation of psalms, the Shema with blessings before and after it, the blessings of the *Amidah*, and Torah readings. By the generation after the destruction of the Temple, the synagogue service was quite well established, although there was not yet a single prayerbook that recorded all of the prayers that were in use.

By the Middle Ages (800 c.e.), differences in the service varied from place to place. Communities were often beholden to the academies in Babylon and Jerusalem for legal advice related to issues of prayer.

The volume that Jewish history has judged as the first

true prayerbook (*siddur*, in Hebrew) was that of Rav Amram, the Gaon of the Sura Academy in Babylon (865 c.e.). Jewish scholars in Spain had appealed to him to supply them with a guide to the correct order of the prayer service. His response to this request became, in essence, the first complete written prayerbook. It contained the regular prayers, according to the order of the whole year—weekdays, Sabbath, the New Moon, fast days, Hanukkah, Purim, and all the festivals—together with the relevant laws preceding each section. At the end of the book were blessings and special prayers for life-cycle events such as circumcision, redemption of the firstborn, marriage, and the burial service.

Approximately one hundred years later, another prayerbook was born—that of Saadia, the Gaon of the Sura Academy. This book was a collection and arrangement of established prayers and blessings. Also included in this prayerbook were many new liturgical prayers by leading scholars of the time. A very old manuscript of Saadia's original prayerbook was discovered in Fayyum, the Egyptian city in which he was born. Another prayerbook was compiled in the eleventh century by Rav Hai ben Sherira Gaon.

In the eleventh century, Rabbi Simcha ben Shmuel, a student of Rashi, the famous Bible commentator, completed a prayerbook called the *Machzor Vitry (The Cycle of Prayers from Vitry)*. This book contained the text of all of the regular prayers, in accordance with the customs present in northern France, as well as a collection of laws of prayer that preceded each section. It served as the basis for the Ashkenazic mode of prayer.

With the advent of the printing press, prayerbooks for different communities were printed in Germany, Spain,

and France. In 1868, Seligman Baer, a German-Jewish
scholar, published a definitive text of the prayerbook. He
had meticulously compared all of the manuscript versions available and traced all the prayers back to their
original talmudic sources. Baer's corrected texts of the
prayerbook are used in most of the recent traditional
prayerbooks published.

PRAYERBOOK TRANSLATIONS

Until the nineteenth century, Jews were mainly concerned with having as correct a version of their prayerbook as possible. Thus, new liturgy continued to be
added, including supplications and penitential prayers.
Translations of prayerbooks began to emerge in the
sixteenth century. One book written especially for women
was that by Elijah Levita, who translated the prayerbook
into Judeo-German, an early form of Yiddish. Since that
time, the number and variety of translations has increased,
with translations in Italian, Spanish, Yiddish, French, German, English, Dutch, Polish, and Russian, just to name a
few. Among the better-known translations of the prayerbooks in English is the *Authorized Prayer Book* (1890) by
S. Singer.

REFORM PRAYERBOOKS

The first published Reform prayerbook appeared in
Germany in 1818, containing both a Hebrew text and its
German translation. The book opened to the left, thus
underscoring the primacy of German. Keeping true to
the theology of Reform Judaism, all references to the

ancient Temple service, sacrifices, the Messiah, and the restoration of Israel to Zion were eliminated. In 1895, *The Union Prayer Book for Jewish Worship* was edited and published by the Central Conference of American Rabbis, the first organization of the Reform Rabbinate in America. This book restored some of the original Hebrew that had been removed in earlier versions. In 1940, the *Union Prayer Book* was revised, with more Hebrew added to the book.

The newest Reform prayerbook, called the *Gates of Prayer*, was published in 1975. It was modeled after, and borrows much from, *Service of the Heart* (London, 1967), the first comprehensive post-World War II prayerbook of Reform Jewry. This newest prayerbook entry contains many optional prayers and meditations. It also includes a section on special themes (nature, humanity, loneliness, trust, sincerity, righteousness, and revelation, to name a few). The prayerbook has at its end a wide variety of songs and hymns.

CONSERVATIVE PRAYERBOOKS

In 1927, the United Synagogue of America published the *Festival Prayerbook*. The aim of this book was to "endow the traditional Jewish service with all the beauty and dignity befitting it and inherent therein." This involved presenting a satisfactory English translation and an accurate Hebrew text, and devoting careful attention to layout and design. The book's English translation allowed for responsive reading as well. In 1946, the Rabbinical Assembly of America and the United Synagogue of America published the *Sabbath and Festival*

Prayerbook. Its guiding principles, mentioned in the book's preface, included continuity with tradition, relevance to the needs of the modern generation, and, intellectual integrity. This prayerbook included many supplementary readings in its appendix.

In 1949, the Hebrew Publishing Company published Philip Birnbaum's *Daily Prayerbook*. Translated and annotated by Birnbaum, it contains an updated English translation with a running commentary to explain various points of interest throughout the prayerbook. Professors Louis Ginzberg, Alexander Marx, Saul Lieberman, Boaz Cohen, Abraham Joshua Heschel, and Simon Greenberg were among those acknowledged by the author for their advice and counsel. Two years after his publication of the *Daily Prayerbook*, Birnbaum published a *Machzor* for Rosh Hashanah and Yom Kippur.

In 1951, a prayerbook called *The High Holiday Prayer Book* (edited by Rabbi Morris Silverman) was published. Recognizing the need of more congregational participation in the service as conducive to greater interest, a number of the English translations were arranged in prose and metrical form for responsive reading.

In 1957, Ben Zion Bokser, a rabbi serving a Conservative synagogue in Queens, New York, published *HaSiddur—The Prayerbook*. This prayerbook, published by the Hebrew Publishing Company, addressed itself to the individual's need for personal prayer in addition to the formal worship requirements of the synagogue. It also added the text of the Book of Esther with a new English translation and commentary.

In 1972, a new High-Holiday prayerbook, *Machzor for Rosh HaShanah and Yom Kippur* (edited by Rabbi Jules Harlow), was published. An updated English translation was presented in this prayerbook, as well as explanatory notes to the text.

In 1991, the Prayer Book Press of Media Judaica, Inc. published *Siddur Hadash* for Sabbath and Festival morning services. It was compiled and edited by Rabbis Sidney Greenberg and Jonathan D. Levine, with companion volumes titled *Likrat Shabbat* for Sabbath and Festival evenings and *Minchat Shabbat* for Sabbath and Festival afternoons. These prayerbooks augment the Hebrew liturgy by presenting the worshipper with new prayers, thoughtful notes, and contemporary meditations. Special material for Festivals and holidays and prayers for important life occasions of both individual and community are presented in clear and readable form.

The newest addition to Conservative prayerbooks is *Sim Shalom*. This book is the most comprehensive of all of the prayerbooks published to date within the Conservative movement. It includes services for the Sabbath, Festivals, and weekdays, as well as texts for various other occasions at home and in the synagogue, and a rabbinic text for study, *Ethics of the Fathers*. The text of this prayerbook also includes options and alternatives for various passages.

ORTHODOX PRAYERBOOKS

Because there are so many varieties of traditional synagogues, there is no single standard prayerbook for the Orthodox movement. However, two prayerbooks published specifically for the traditional Orthodox community continue to be quite popular.

Perhaps considered the most authoritative prayerbook in the so-called modern Orthodox world is *The Tradi-*

tional Prayerbook for Sabbath and Festivals, edited and translated by David De Sola Pool under the direction of the *Siddur Committee* of the Rabbinical Council of America. Published by Behrman House, it also includes hymns and prayers for various occasions in the synagogue, home prayers and rituals, and the Torah readings for Festivals.

In 1984, the extremely popular prayerbook, *The Complete ArtScroll Siddur*, was published by Mesorah Publications. Translated and with an anthologized commentary by Rabbi Nosson Scherman, this comprehensive prayerbook includes blessings and prayers for all imaginable occasions. The commentary is quite skillfully written, and helps to enhance one's understanding of the prayers.

RECONSTRUCTIONIST PRAYERBOOK

The early Reconstructionist prayerbooks, including *Seder Tefillot le-Shabbat— Sabbath Prayer Book* (1945), *Mahzor le-Yamim Noraim— High Holy Day Prayer Book* (1948), *Festival Prayer Book* (1958), and *Seder Tefillot li-Y'mot ha-Hol— Daily Prayer Book* (1963), reduced the repetition of the traditional prayers to a minimum, contracted some prayers, and eliminated others. Like the early Reform prayerbooks, the Reconstructionist prayerbooks have omitted all references to an individual Messiah, to sacrifices, to the Priests and Levites, and to the doctrine of bodily resurrection. In addition, prayers that implied Israel's superiority over other peoples were either excised or changed. The Reconstructionist prayerbook also has substituted its own formula for the traditional Torah service blessings.

The newest and latest addition to the Reconstructionist prayerbooks is that called *Kol Haneshamah* (chairperson David A. Teutsch). Readings in the prayerbook have been selected with attention to literary quality and clarity. The book includes a fresh English translation, guiding meditations, songs, transliteration, and prayer commentary.

GENRES OF PRAYER

Prayers in the prayerbook come in various fixed forms. This chapter will explore three categories of prayers: the blessing, the *piyyut*, and the psalm.

BLESSINGS

Forms of Blessings

The building block of all Jewish prayer is the blessing. This liturgical formula referring to the praise of God is the main source of all of the poetry that was composed and added to the prayerbook over the centuries. The blessings pronounced on various occasions are attributed to the men of the Great Assembly (400 to 300 B.C.E.), the spiritual leaders in the time of Ezra the Scribe, who are considered to be the successors of the prophets in that they kept alive the knowledge of the Torah and Jewish traditions. Blessings were formulated for practically every contingency: for the usual experiences of daily life, such as arising from sleep, dressing, eating, and drinking, and for the unusual happenings, such as escaping from danger, recovering from illness, or seeing something wondrous in nature.

The Hebrew word for blessing, *berachah*, is generally understood to be derived from the Hebrew word *berech* ("knee"). The bending of the knee while praying was one of the ways of honoring God. The Rashba, a talmudic scholar (*Teshuvot* 5:51), states that the word *berachah* is derived from the Hebrew word *braichah*, which means "spring" (of water). Just as a spring flows constantly and its waters increase, so, too, when we bless God we are proclaiming our desire to display God's ever-increasing presence in the world. As to the number of blessings required for daily recitation, it was Rabbi Meir, a second-century scholar, who stated that it is the duty of every Jew to recite one hundred blessings daily.

Blessings come in many different forms. The shortest form is *Baruch ata Adonai* ("Blessed is the Lord"). King David is quoted as saying, "Blessed are You, Lord" (1 Chronicles 29:10), a phrase that eventually became an important key to the prayer. A second form of the blessing is *Baruch ata Adonai Eloheinu melech ha'olam* ("Praised are You, O Lord, Sovereign of the universe"). The model for this phrase may have been the opening line of the Shema, "Hear O Israel, the Lord our God, the Lord is One" (Deuteronomy 6:4).

The longest form is for those blessings that are recited in conjunction with the performance of a specific religious obligation (*mitzvah*). It adds the phrase *asher kidshanu b'mitzvotav v'tzivanu* ("who sanctified us with His commandments and commanded us to. . . ."). One interesting feature of this longer blessing formula is the switch within the blessing from second-person voice to third-person. At the beginning, God is addressed directly: "Blessed are You." This is immediately followed by a change of the person of the blessing from second to third, when speaking about God: "who sanctified us with *His* commandments." This change allows for the realization on the part of the person uttering the blessing that God is both near and far—or, in theological terms, both "immanent" and "transcendent." Abudarham, a fourteenth-century scholar, relates the use of both the second and third person in the blessing to the hidden and revealed aspects of God. To that which God reveals, we use the more familiar second person, while the third-person voice reminds us that God's essence will always remain a mystery.

Purposes of Blessings

The genius of the blessing formula is the opportunity it provides for the worshipper to establish a close relationship with God by speaking to Him directly. Steve Brown, in his book *Higher and Higher: Making Prayer a Part of Us* (United Synagogue Department of Youth), identifies several important purposes of the blessing formula:

To thank God for the blessings that a person has received.

To assume an ethical responsibility for our blessings. For example, when one recites a blessing thank-

ing God for giving bread, there ought to be an
expectation of taking on an ethical responsibility
for one's food, which would include that of not
wasting food.

To help sensitize people to the beauty and joy of the
world that God has given people. By saying
"thank you" to God for one's blessings, a person
does not take life and life's blessings for granted.

To help embue an experience with spirituality. Reciting blessings helps a person to change the common variety of experience, raising it, and, in the
process, making a person closer to the image of
God.

Kinds of Blessings

Maimonides, the medieval philosopher, distinguishes
three kinds of benedictions according to their content:
those recited before and after the enjoyment of a pleasure, such as eating; those preceding the performance of
certain religious duties, such as listening to the *shofar*
(ram's horn); and those that are forms of thanksgiving
and praise. The blessings of the morning, which express
a person's gratitude for awakening in possession of all
his or her faculties, were originally of the third type.
Many of the benedictions in these three categories,
though obligatory, are essentially of a private character.
Accordingly, no *minyan* (quorum) is required for their
recital. An exception is the Grace After Meals, which,
when said in company, is preceded by an invitation to
those present to offer their thanks in unison.

Here is a summary of the major blessings, listed by
category.

Blessings for Taste

Bread

בָּרוּךְ אַתָּה יהוה אֱלֹהֵינוּ מֶלֶךְ הָעוֹלָם, הַמּוֹצִיא לֶחֶם מִן הָאָרֶץ.

Blessed are You, O Lord our God, Sovereign of the universe, who brings forth bread from the earth.

Baruch ata Adonai Eloheinu melech ha'olam hamotzi lechem min ha'aretz.

Food (other than bread) prepared from wheat, barley, rye, oats, or spelt

בָּרוּךְ אַתָּה יהוה אֱלֹהֵינוּ מֶלֶךְ הָעוֹלָם, בּוֹרֵא מִינֵי מְזוֹנוֹת.

Blessed are You, O Lord our God, Sovereign of the universe, who creates different kinds of nourishment.

Baruch ata Adonai Eloheinu melech ha'olam borei meienei mezonot.

Wine

בָּרוּךְ אַתָּה יהוה אֱלֹהֵינוּ מֶלֶךְ הָעוֹלָם, בּוֹרֵא פְּרִי הַגָּפֶן.

Blessed are You, O Lord our God, Sovereign of the universe, who creates the fruit of the vine.

Baruch ata Adonai Eloheinu melech ha'olam borei p'ri hagafen.

Fruit

בָּרוּךְ אַתָּה יהוה אֱלֹהֵינוּ מֶלֶךְ הָעוֹלָם, בּוֹרֵא פְּרִי הָעֵץ.

Blessed are You, O Lord our God, Sovereign of the universe, who creates the fruit of the tree.

Baruch ata Adonai Eloheinu melekh ha'olam borei p'ri ha'eitz.

Foods that grow in the ground

בָּרוּךְ אַתָּה יהוה אֱלֹהֵינוּ מֶלֶךְ הָעוֹלָם, בּוֹרֵא פְּרִי הָאֲדָמָה.

Blessed are You, O Lord our God, Sovereign of the universe, who creates the fruit of the ground.

Baruch ata Adonai Eloheinu melech ha'olam borei p'ri ha'adamah.

Other food and drink

בָּרוּךְ אַתָּה יהוה אֱלֹהֵינוּ מֶלֶךְ הָעוֹלָם, שֶׁהַכֹּל נִהְיָה בִּדְבָרוֹ.

Blessed are You, O Lord our God, Sovereign of the universe, at whose word all things come into existence.

Baruch ata Adonai Eloheinu melech ha'olam shehakol nihiyeh bidvaro.

Blessings for Smell

Upon smelling fragrant spices

בָּרוּךְ אַתָּה יהוה אֱלֹהֵינוּ מֶלֶךְ הָעוֹלָם, בּוֹרֵא מִינֵי בְשָׂמִים.

Blessed are You, O Lord our God, Sovereign of the universe, who creates different kinds of spices.

Baruch ata Adonai Eloheinu melech ha'olam borei minei besamim.

Upon smelling the fragrance of shrubs and trees

בָּרוּךְ אַתָּה יהוה אֱלֹהֵינוּ מֶלֶךְ הָעוֹלָם, בּוֹרֵא עֲצֵי בְשָׂמִים.

Blessed are You, O Lord our God, Sovereign of the universe, who creates fragrant trees.

Baruch ata Adonai Eloheinu melech ha'olam borei atzei besamim.

Upon smelling the fragrance of plants and herbs

בָּרוּךְ אַתָּה יהוה אֱלֹהֵינוּ מֶלֶךְ הָעוֹלָם, בּוֹרֵא עִשְׂבֵי בְשָׂמִים.

Blessed are You, O Lord our God, Sovereign of the universe, who creates fragrant plants.

Baruch ata Adonai Eloheinu melech ha'olam borei isvei besamim.

Upon smelling fragrant fruit

בָּרוּךְ אַתָּה יהוה אֱלֹהֵינוּ מֶלֶךְ הָעוֹלָם, הַנּוֹתֵן רֵיחַ טוֹב בַּפֵּרוֹת.

Blessed are You, O Lord our God, Sovereign of the universe, who gives a pleasant fragrance to fruits.

Baruch ata Adonai Eloheinu melech ha'olam hanoteyn rei'ach tov ba'peyrot.

Upon smelling fragrant oils

בָּרוּךְ אַתָּה יהוה אֱלֹהֵינוּ מֶלֶךְ הָעוֹלָם, בּוֹרֵא שֶׁמֶן עָרֵב.

Blessed are You, O Lord our God, Sovereign of the universe, who creates fragrant oil.

Baruch ata Adonai Eloheinu melech ha'olam borei shemen areyv.

Blessings for Sight

Upon seeing a rainbow

בָּרוּךְ אַתָּה יהוה אֱלֹהֵינוּ מֶלֶךְ הָעוֹלָם, זוֹכֵר הַבְּרִית וְנֶאֱמָן בִּבְרִיתוֹ וְקַיָּם בְּמַאֲמָרוֹ.

Blessed are You, O Lord our God, Sovereign of the universe, who remembers the covenant and is faithful to all promises.

Baruch ata Adonai Eloheinu melech ha'olam zocher ha'berit vene'eman bivrito vekayam bema'amaro.

Upon seeing trees blossoming for the first time in the year

בָּרוּךְ אַתָּה יהוה אֱלֹהֵינוּ מֶלֶךְ הָעוֹלָם, שֶׁלֹּא חִסֵּר בְּעוֹלָמוֹ דָּבָר, וּבְרָא בוֹ בְּרִיּוֹת טוֹבוֹת וְאִילָנוֹת טוֹבִים לְהַנּוֹת בָּהֶם בְּנֵי אָדָם.

Blessed are You, O Lord our God, Sovereign of the universe, Who has withheld nothing from the world and Who has created lovely creatures and beautiful trees for people to enjoy.

Baruch ata Adonai Eloheinu melech ha'olam shelo chisar be'olamo davar uvara vo briyot tovot ve'ilanot tovim lehanot baheym benei adam.

Upon seeing the ocean

בָּרוּךְ אַתָּה יהוה אֱלֹהֵינוּ מֶלֶךְ הָעוֹלָם, שֶׁעָשָׂה אֶת־הַיָּם הַגָּדוֹל.

Blessed are You, O Lord our God, Sovereign of the universe, who has made the great sea.

Baruch ata Adonai Eloheinu melech ha'olam she'asah et hayam hagadol.

Upon seeing trees or creatures of unusual beauty

בָּרוּךְ אַתָּה יהוה אֱלֹהֵינוּ מֶלֶךְ הָעוֹלָם, שֶׁכָּכָה לוֹ בְּעוֹלָמוֹ.

Blessed are You, O Lord our God, Sovereign of the universe, who has such beauty in the world.

Baruch ata Adonai Eloheinu melech ha'olam sheka-khah lo be'olamo.

Upon seeing someone of abnormal appearance

בָּרוּךְ אַתָּה יהוה אֱלֹהֵינוּ מֶלֶךְ הָעוֹלָם, מְשַׁנֶּה הַבְּרִיּוֹת.

Blessed are You, O Lord our God, Sovereign of the universe, who makes people different.

Baruch ata Adonai Eloheinu melech ha'olam meshaneh habriyot.

Upon seeing lightning, shooting stars, mountains, or a sunrise

בָּרוּךְ אַתָּה יהוה אֱלֹהֵינוּ מֶלֶךְ הָעוֹלָם, עֹשֶׂה מַעֲשֵׂה בְרֵאשִׁית.

Blessed are You, O Lord our God, Sovereign of the universe, Source of creation.

Baruch ata Adonai Eloheinu melech ha'olam oseh ma'aseh veresheet.

Upon seeing a synagogue restored

בָּרוּךְ אַתָּה יהוה אֱלֹהֵינוּ מֶלֶךְ הָעוֹלָם, מַצִּיב גְּבוּל אַלְמָנָה.

Blessed are You, O Lord our God, Sovereign of the universe, who restores the borders of the widow [Zion].

Baruch ata Adonai Eloheinu melech ha'olam matziv gevul almanah.

Upon seeing a person distinguished in Torah knowledge

בָּרוּךְ אַתָּה יהוה אֱלֹהֵינוּ מֶלֶךְ הָעוֹלָם, שֶׁחָלַק מֵחָכְמָתוֹ לִירֵאָיו.

Blessed are You, O Lord our God, Sovereign of the universe, who has given wisdom to those who revere God.

Baruch ata Adonai Eloheinu melech ha'olam shechalak meichokhmato lirei'av.

Upon seeing a person distinguished in secular knowledge

בָּרוּךְ אַתָּה יהוה אֱלֹהֵינוּ מֶלֶךְ הָעוֹלָם, שֶׁנָּתַן מֵחָכְמָתוֹ לְבָשָׂר וָדָם.

Blessed are You, O Lord our God, Sovereign of the universe, who has given wisdom to mortals.

Baruch ata Adonai Eloheinu melech ha'olam shenatan mechokhmato levasar vadam.

Upon seeing a head of state

בָּרוּךְ אַתָּה יהוה אֱלֹהֵינוּ מֶלֶךְ הָעוֹלָם, שֶׁנָּתַן מִכְּבוֹדוֹ לְבָשָׂר וָדָם.

Blessed are You, O Lord our God, Sovereign of the universe, who has given glory to mortals.

Baruch ata Adonai Eloheinu melech ha'olam shenatan mikvodo levasar vadam.

Upon seeing a friend after a long separation

בָּרוּךְ אַתָּה יהוה אֱלֹהֵינוּ מֶלֶךְ הָעוֹלָם, מְחַיֵה הַמֵתִים.

Blessed are You, O Lord our God, Sovereign of the universe, who brings the dead back to life.

Baruch ata Adonai Eloheinu melech ha'olam mechayeh hameytim.

Blessing upon Hearing

Upon hearing thunder

בָּרוּךְ אַתָּה יהוה אֱלֹהֵינוּ מֶלֶךְ הָעוֹלָם, שֶׁכֹּחוֹ וּגְבוּרָתוֹ מָלֵא עוֹלָם.

Blessed are You, O Lord our God, Sovereign of the universe, whose might and power fill the entire world.

Baruch ata Adonai Eloheinu melech ha'olam shekocho ugevarato malei olam.

Upon hearing good news

בָּרוּךְ אַתָּה יהוה אֱלֹהֵינוּ מֶלֶךְ הָעוֹלָם, הַטוֹב וְהַמֵּטִיב.

Blessed are You, O Lord our God, Sovereign of the universe, who is good and causes good things.

Baruch ata Adonai Eloheinu melech ha'olam hatov vehameytiv.

Upon hearing tragic news

בָּרוּךְ אַתָּה יהוה אֱלֹהֵינוּ מֶלֶךְ הָעוֹלָם, דַּיַּן הָאֱמֶת.

Blessed are You, O Lord our God, Sovereign of the universe, who is the true Judge.

Baruch ata Adonai Eloheinu melech ha'olam dayan ha'emet.

Other Blessings of Gratitude

After leaving the bathroom

בָּרוּךְ אַתָּה יהוה אֱלֹהֵינוּ מֶלֶךְ הָעוֹלָם, אֲשֶׁר יָצַר אֶת הָאָדָם בְּחָכְמָה וּבָרָא בּוֹ
נְקָבִים נְקָבִים חֲלוּלִים חֲלוּלִים. גָּלוּי וְיָדוּעַ לִפְנֵי כִסֵּא כְבוֹדֶךָ שֶׁאִם יִפָּתֵחַ אֶחָד
מֵהֶם אוֹ יִסָּתֵם אֶחָד מֵהֶם אִי אֶפְשָׁר לְהִתְקַיֵּם וְלַעֲמוֹד לְפָנֶיךָ. בָּרוּךְ אַתָּה יהוה
רוֹפֵא כָל בָּשָׂר וּמַפְלִיא לַעֲשׂוֹת.

Blessed are You, O Lord our God, Sovereign of the universe, who has formed people in wisdom and created in them many orifices and hollow tubes. It is well known that if one of them were to be obstructed or broken, it would be impossible to stay alive. Blessed are You, Healer of all flesh, who does wondrous things.

Baruch ata Adonai Eloheinu melech ha'olam asher yatzar et ha'adam bechachma uvara vo nikavim nikavim chalulim chalulim galui veyadua lifnei kisei kevodecha she'im yipate'ach echad meihem oh yisatem echad meihem ee'efshar lehitkayem vela'amod lifanecha. Baruch ata Adonai rofei koi basar umaflee la'asot.

Upon affixing a mezuzah to the doorpost

בָּרוּךְ אַתָּה יהוה אֱלֹהֵינוּ מֶלֶךְ הָעוֹלָם, אֲשֶׁר קִדְּשָׁנוּ בְּמִצְוֹתָיו וְצִוָּנוּ לִקְבּוֹעַ מְזוּזָה.

Blessed are You, O Lord our God, Sovereign of the
universe, who has made us distinct with commandments
and commanded us to attach the *mezuzah.*

*Baruch ata Adonai Eloheinu melech ha'olam asher
kid-shanu bemitzvotav vetzivanu likboah mezuzah.*

*Upon obtaining a new item, tasting a new food for the
first time, entering a new home, and many other new
and special occasions*

בָּרוּךְ אַתָּה יהוה אֱלֹהֵינוּ מֶלֶךְ הָעוֹלָם, שֶׁהֶחֱיָנוּ וְקִיְּמָנוּ וְהִגִּיעָנוּ לַזְּמָן הַזֶּה.

Blessed are You, O Lord our God, Sovereign of the
universe, who has given us life, sustained us, and helped
us to reach this day.

*Baruch ata Adonai Eloheinu melech ha'olam shehechey-
anu vikimanu vihigiyanu lazman hazeh.*

Notable Blessing Quotations

A variety of statements related to blessings have been
presented over the centuries. Here is a selection of some
of them.

1. The person who utters blessings is blessed. One who
   utters curses is cursed (Ruth Rabbah 1:3).

2. Israel enjoys blessings in this world because of the
   blessings of Bilaam, but the blessings wherewith the

Patriarchs have blessed them are preserved for the World-to-Come (Deuteronomy Rabbah 3:4).

3. A person should taste nothing before uttering a blessing. Since "the earth is the Lord's, and all that it holds" [Psalms 24:1], a person embezzles from God when making use of this world without uttering a blessing (Tosefta *Berachot* 4:1).

4. Rabbi Yose says: "The person who changes the formulas the sages have fixed for blessings has not discharged his duty" (Tosefta *Berachot* 4:4–5).

5. Let not the blessing of a lay person be light in your eyes (*Berachot* 7a).

6. From a person's blessings, one may know if one is or is not a scholar. (*Berachot* 50a).

7. Just as one has to bless God for the good, one has to bless God for the bad (*Berachot* 48b).

8. There is no vessel that holds blessedness more securely than peace (Jerusalem Talmud, *Berachot* 2:4).

PIYYUTIM

The History of *Piyyutim*

Although the word *piyyut* is derived from the Greek term for poetry, it generally denotes religious poetry; hence, *payyetan* signifies a liturgical poet. In ancient times, these liturgical compositions were intended to replace or substitute for many of the set versions of prayer. Although the majority of *piyyutim* were intended to be used during the major Jewish holy days, some were reproduced for the Sabbath or weekdays.

Piyyut literature began in Israel while the various versions of the obligatory prayers were being established. Texts of ancient *piyyutim* are found in scattered talmudic sources.

One of the earliest *piyyut* writers known to us by name was Yose ben Yose, who lived and worked in Israel in approximately the sixth century. Other important payyetanim of this era include Yannai, Simeon ben Megas, Elliezer be Kallir, Chaduta ben Abraham, and Joshua HaKohen. In the ninth century, *piyyutim* began to flourish in southern Italy, and by the end of the tenth century, liturgical activity had spread to North Africa. The most important region of central European liturgical poetry was Germany, whose great poets included the likes of Moses ben Kalonymus, Meshullam ben Kalonymus, and Simeon ben Isaac.

In the middle of the tenth century, several great liturgical composers emerged, included Judah Halevi, Abraham ibn Ezra, and Solomon ibn Gabirol, whom some say wrote the famous poem *Adon Olam* (Master of the Universe). The thirteenth century marked the beginning of the decline of *piyyut* productivity.

Israel Davidson, a scholar who devoted a lifetime to the classification and identification of extant *piyyutim*, lists in his *Thesaurus of Medieval Hebrew Poetry* over 34,000 hymns by some three thousand authors!

The *Kerovah Piyyut*

Piyyutim can be divided into a number of categories. One of the most important and earliest types of liturgical poems was the *kerovah*. The *kerovah* was designed to be included in the *Amidah* prayer for Festivals and distinguished Sabbaths. When the cantor repeats the earlier part of the *Amidah* aloud, the *kerovot* are recited responsively or alternately. The term *kerovot* is derived from the Hebrew verb *karov* (meaning "to approach"); that is, the cantor approaches the Holy Ark and offers petitions on behalf of the worshippers.

The *kerovot* are divided into a number of secondary categories according to the types of *Amidah* to which they are attached. Each has its own structural characteristics. For instance, there is the *kerovah* of the daily *Amidah*, called the *kerovat Shemoneh Esrei* because of the eighteen blessings in that *Amidah*. The *kerovah* of the *Musaf* (additional service) for the Sabbath and Festivals is called *shivata* because of the seven (in Hebrew, *shevah*) blessings in these *Amidah* prayers. The *kerovah* of the morning Sabbath and Festival *Amidah*, which includes a *Kedushah* (prayer of sanctification), is called *kedushata*.

Among the *kerovot* of the major Jewish Festivals, a number of specialized liturgical poems are found. These include the *tefi'ata* that adorn the *malchuyot* ("sovereignty"), *zichronot* ("remembrance"), and *shofarot* ("ram's horn") blessings in the *Musaf* Amidah for the Jewish New Year. The *kerovot* for Jewish fast days include *selichot* (penitential poems). A secondary type of penitential liturgical poem was the *pizmon* ("refrain"), which included a musical refrain that was often chanted by the worshippers together with the reader. The special *kerovot* for the Fast of the Ninth of Av included *kinot* (dirges). *Selichot* were also composed for the Days of Penitence during the month of Elul and for use during the Ten Days of Repentance (i.e., the days between Rosh Hashanah and Yom Kippur). Specialized poems used during the processionals on the Festival of Sukkot are called *hoshanah* ("save me") *piyyutim*.

All of the aforementioned poetical insertions have helped to create the refreshing atmosphere of each Jewish Festival.

The *Yotzer Piyyut*

A second type of *piyyut* is called the *yotzer*. This specialized *piyyut* was designed for insertion within the framework of the Shema prayer during the Festival morning (*Shachari*) service. The term *yotzer* is derived from the Hebrew phrase *yotzer ohr* ("Creator of light") used in the *yotzer* blessing that precedes the Shema. It emphasizes the goodness of God, the Creator of light, who daily renews creation. The *yotzer* poems were especially prevalent between the seventh and eleventh centuries.

Parallel to the *yotzer* poems, which were intended for the morning service, were *piyyutim* of the evening, which adorned the blessings before and after the evening Shema prayer. This type of liturgical poem was not widely circulated.

The Language and Style of *Piyyutim*

The style and vocabulary of the various liturgical poets vary from period to period. During the earliest period of the *piyyut*, the vocabulary was usually biblical, with little wordplay and no use of rhyme. Over time, the vocabulary of the *piyyutim* became more diverse, with inclusion of talmudic and midrashic material as well as a more expansive Hebrew vocabulary using rhyme and rhythm. The Spanish liturgists introduced a precise method of both rhythm and rhyme in their poems.

THE STRUCTURE OF THE PRAYER SERVICE

Having looked at the development of the prayerbook and the structure of the blessing upon which most prayers are based, we can now begin to examine the structure of the individual prayer services.

The Jewish liturgy evolved over many centuries. It is remarkable that all morning services for each day of the year continue to have the same basic structure, with allowance for additions or modifications based upon the cycle of the Jewish year. This is also true for the afternoon and evening services. This sacred structure is known as the *matbe'ah shel tefillah* (literally, the "'official stamp' of the prayer service").

The beginnings of a sacred order to the prayer service can be found in the talmudic Tractate *Berachot*, which deals in part with the prayer and worship of Israel and the regulations relating to the main components of daily prayers. Prescribed Jewish worship consists of three daily services: *Shacharit* (morning), *Mincha* (afternoon), and *Ma'ariv* (evening). On the Sabbath and Festivals, *Musaf* (additional service) traditionally follows the *Shacharit*. At the beginning of the Sabbath, the *Kabbalat Shabbat* ("welcoming of the Sabbath") service precedes the evening service. Each service contains an *Amidah* (literally, "standing prayer"), the central prayer, with much of the liturgy built around it. In traditional synagogues (including some Conservative synagogues), the *Amidah* is first read silently by the worshippers and then is repeated aloud by the leader of the service, except for the evening service. The Shema prayer (a recitation of three sections of the Torah) and its special accompanying blessings are recited prior to the *Amidah* at both morning and evening services.

Shacharit is preceded by a preliminary service, a sort of prelude to the prayer service itself. It consists of a collection of morning blessings, called *Birchot haShachar*, and *pesukei d'Zimra* (Verses of Song), a collection of biblical prayers from Psalms and elsewhere. *Mincha* has a brief preliminary section consisting of Psalm 145 and a few other verses. Following the weekday *Shacharit Amidah* and *Mincha Amidah*, *Tachanun* (supplicatory prayers) is recited. In the *Shacharit* service *Tachanun* is followed by several psalms and a prayer called *Kedushah d'Sidra* ("a prayer of sanctification"). The different sections of the prayer service are separated by a recital of Kaddish, a prayer that praises God's name. Various forms of the Kaddish prayer appear at the conclusion of the preliminary service, the Torah reading, after *Shacharit*, and after *Musaf*.

Each Monday, Thursday, Sabbath, and Festival, the

Torah is read following the completion of the *Shacharit Amidah*. On special holidays, *Hallel* (psalms of praise to God) is recited, while standing, immediately after the *Shacharit Amidah*. Each service concludes with *Aleynu*, a prayer in which God's universal power and the particularism of the Jewish people are articulated.

Although the specific content of the prayers changes with the occasion, they always consist of three main categories of prayer: praise of God, prayers of thanksgiving, and prayers of petition.

The following outlines the daily *Shacharit* morning service:

Birchot haShachar (early-morning blessings)
Selected psalms
Yishtabach
Barechu ("call to prayer")
First blessing before the Shema—*Yotzer ohr* (God creates light anew each day)
Second blessing before the Shema—*Ahava Rabbah* (God gives us the Torah and shows us love)
The Shema—three   Deuteronomy 6:5–9
    paragraphs: Deuteronomy 11:13–21
                     Numbers 15:37–41
Blessing after the Shema—*Ga'al Yisrael* (God redeems Israel)
Amidah
Torah reading (Mondays and Thursdays)
Kaddish *Shalem* (Full Kaddish)
Aleynu
Kaddish *Yatom* (Mourner's Kaddish)

The following is an outline of the *Mincha* (afternoon) service:

Ashrei (Psalm 145)
Uva letzion go'el ("There comes a redeemer"; on the Sabbath and Festivals)
Chatzi Kaddish (Half Kaddish)
Torah reading (on the Sabbath and fast days)
Chatzi Kaddish (Half Kaddish)
Amidah
Kaddish *Shalem* (Full Kaddish)
Aleynu
Kaddish *Yatom* (Mourner's Kaddish)

The following is an outline of the daily *Ma'ariv* (evening) service:

Barechu
First blessing before the Shema
Second blessing before the Shema
The three paragraphs of the Shema
Mi Kamocha
First blessing after the Shema
Second blessing after the Shema
Chatzi Kaddish (Half Kaddish)
Amidah
Kaddish *Shalem* (Full Kaddish)
Aleynu
Kaddish *Yatom* (Mourner's Kaddish)

TIMES FOR PRAYER

Just as the number of prayer services was fixed each day, so, too, did the rabbis fix the time framework in which to say them. The official time for the various services was instituted to correspond to the time that the daily communal offerings were brought in the Temple. These periods continue to provide the basic framework within which these various prayers may be recited. Of course, the local rabbi is a person's final authority, since different communities may have different customs. In addition, one's location is affected by the times of sunrise and sunset, which must always be taken into account when scheduling the precise time of a particular service.

The rabbis of bygone years, when referring to the time of day, were not referring to a fixed hour. Rather, they referred to a certain fraction of the day, and the hour they had in mind was a "variable" or "seasonal" hour (in Hebrew, *sha-ah zemanit*), whose length is determined by the length of a day measured from sunrise to sunset, which itself varies according to the seasons. The one constant of a variable hour is that it is always one-twelfth of the day. Thus, for example, the fourth hour is always one-third of a day. Knowing this structure, one can now understand the following guidelines for the times of each prayer service.

Time for the Morning (*Shacharit*) Service

According to the *Code of Jewish Law* (Orach Chayyim 443), the time frame within which the morning service should be recited begins at sunrise and lasts until the end of the fourth hour, which is equivalent to one-third of the day. Since in ancient times the daily offering could be brought as early as dawn, one could begin the *Amidah* as early as the crack of dawn. Although the proper time requirement is not met if a person prays after the fourth-hour deadline, the morning service may be said through the sixth hour, which still fulfills the prayer requirement.

Time for the Afternoon (*Mincha*) Service

The preferred time for saying the *Mincha* (afternoon) service is nine-and-one-half-hours into the day until sundown, for it was during this time that the *Mincha* offering was brought. When said during this period, the service is called *Mincha ketanah* ("short" *Mincha*) because the time period of two-and-one-half hours during which it is said is quite short.

One may, however, say *Mincha* as early as six-and-one-half hours into the day. When said during the earlier part of the afternoon, the prayer is called *Mincha gedolah* ("long" *Mincha*) because the time until sundown is quite long.

The period between sundown and nightfall is called *bayn hashemashot* (literally, "between the suns"), and is regarded as doubtful night. The Jewish legal definition of night is a minimum of three medium-size stars visible in the sky.

One talmudic sage, Rabbi Judah (*Berachot* 4:1), held the opinion that *Mincha* should be said no later than one-and-one-quarter hours before sundown. Since the standard *Mincha* period begins at two-and-one-half hours before sunset, Rabbi Judah's deadline for *Mincha* is called *pelag haMincha* ("half Mincha"), for it is the halfway mark in that period. The *pelag haMincha* marked the time when, during Temple times, the afternoon sacrificial offering was taken up with other aspects of ritual, such as the burning of the incense.

Today, the general custom is to recite the *Mincha* close to sunset, followed immediately by *Ma'ariv,* so that worshippers don't need to return to the synagogue on two separate occasions.

Time for the Evening (*Ma'ariv*) Service

The time for *Ma'ariv* begins when the time for *Mincha* ends. Those who follow the opinion of Rabbi Judah may say *Ma'ariv* immediately after *pelag haMincha* (i.e., one-and-one-quarter hours before sundown). Those who regularly say *Mincha* until sundown may say *Ma'ariv* right after sundown. The generally preferred practice among traditional Jews is to wait until nightfall for *Ma'ariv.*

Time for the Additional (*Musaf*) Service

Musaf always follows the *Shacharit* service, inasmuch as the ancient *Musaf* sacrificial offering on Sabbaths and Festivals always followed the daily *Shacharit* offering. According to the *Code of Jewish Law* (Orach Chayyim 286:1), the *Musaf* service ought not to be delayed beyond the end of the seventh hour.

Time for the Shema

The time for the Shema prayer was prescribed based upon the rabbinical understanding of the biblical verse "when you lie down and when you rise up" (Deuteronomy 6:7). According to the *Code of Jewish Law* (Orach Chayyim 235:1), one can say the evening Shema no earlier than nightfall. If one says it earlier as part of the evening service conducted before nightfall, then the Shema must be repeated after nightfall.

When a congregation conducts the *Ma'ariv* service earlier than nightfall, it is preferable to say *Ma'ariv* with the congregation rather than saying it privately after nightfall.

The Shema may be said until midnight, a rabbinic deadline established to discourage procrastination. If a delay does occur, one may say the Shema at any time of night before dawn.

The morning Shema may be said as soon as there is enough natural light to recognize an acquaintance at a distance of four cubits (roughly six feet). This is expected to occur at about thirty-five minutes before sunrise. The Shema may be said until the end of the third hour, which is equivalent to one-fourth of the day. When necessary, it may be recited as early as dawn, but it should not be delayed beyond the third hour past sunrise (*Code of Jewish Law*, Orach Chayyim 58:1).

Daily Prayer Synopsis

The following is a synopsis of the prayers of the weekday prayer service. Each prayer is described using the following categories: Background, Concepts, Prayer Motions (if applicable), and Special Recitation Customs (if applicable).

Modeh Ani

I am thankful to You, living, enduring Sovereign One, for restoring my soul to me in compassion. You are dependable beyond measure.

Background

This prayer is customarily said upon first opening the eyes in the morning. The idea behind this prayer (to be said at home) is that a Jew ought to wake up with gratitude to God for having restored one's faculties, and with an enthusiastic desire to serve God. In this way, a person renews a personal covenant with God on a daily basis. This prayer is said to be based on an interpretation of the verse, "They are new each morning, great is Your faithfulness" (Lamentations 3:23).

Concepts

1. We thank God each day for renewing our physical and mental abilities.

2. We praise God for His dependability in maintaining a regular and orderly cycle of nature.

Mah Tovu

How good are your tents, O Jacob, your dwelling places, O Israel.

Background

The *Mah Tovu* prayer consists of a variety of biblical verses (Numbers 24:5; Psalms 5:8, 26:8, 95:6, 69:14) that express one's feelings of reverence and joy on entering a synagogue. The opening verse of the prayer was originally recited by Bilaam, a gentile prophet who was hired by Balak, the King of Moab, to put a curse on the Israelites. Seeing their beautifully arranged camps set on a hilltop, Bilaam was so moved that instead of cursing Israel, he blessed them with the words, "How good are your tents, O Jacob, your dwelling places, O Israel." Because Jewish tradition understood the word "tents" to refer to synagogues, and "dwelling places" to refer to schools, it became customary to recite the words of this prayer upon first entering the synagogue.

Concepts

1. This prayer reflects the beauty of praying in a community of worshippers.

2. We must worship God in reverential love and awe. When we appreciate the place in which we are worshipping and feel the love of God, we are then psychologically prepared to proceed with the rest of the prayer service.

Asher Yatzar

Blessed are You, O Lord our God, Ruler of the universe, who has formed human beings in wisdom, creating many passages and vessels. . . . If but one of them is opened or closed, it would be impossible to exist and stand before You . . . .

Background

This ancient prayer, which appears very early in the *siddur*, expresses thankfulness for one's physical health and well-being, and the wondrous laws by which physical health is preserved. The human body is marvelously constructed, and the life of every human being is dependent upon the regular discharge of bodily functions. This prayer is customarily recited by the traditional Jew after having used the bathroom.

Concepts

1. This prayer praises God for creating the wondrous mechanisms of the body and for preserving our health and our lives.

2. This prayer reflects the importance that Judaism attaches to proper health care, reminding us that our bodies are, so to speak, on loan to us from God.

3. This prayer is a reminder that we must do all that is in our power to take proper care of ourselves.

Birchot HaShachar: Blessings of the Morning

Blessed are You, O Lord our God, Ruler of the universe:
   . . . who helps Your creatures distinguish between day and night.
   . . . who made me in God's image.
   . . . who made me a Jew.
   . . . who made me a free person.
   . . . who gives sight to the blind.
   . . . who clothes the naked.
   . . . who releases the downtrodden.
   . . . who creates heaven and earth.
   . . . who provides me with everything.
   . . . who guides us on our path.
   . . . who strengthens Israel with courage.
   . . . who gives Israel glory.
   . . . who restores strength to those who are weary.

Background

This series of fifteen blessings is based on Tractate *Berachot* 60b, where the rabbis teach that as one experiences the phenomena of the new day, one ought to bless God for providing them. Originally, these blessings were said at home when performing one's regular daily morning routine of arising from bed, washing, dressing, and so forth.

In later years, because many people lacked the ability to say these prayers by themselves, they were included in the prayerbook as part of the preliminary morning service.

Concepts

The routine elements in our lives, including our ability to wash and dress ourselves, ought not to be taken for granted. These abilities have been given to us by God, and, in a sense, are daily miracles for which thanks must be given.

Prayer Motions

The *Code of Jewish Law* (Orach Chayyim 46) suggests a variety of actions to accompany the various blessings of the morning.

When hearing the crow of a rooster, one recites the blessing, ". . . who gives the mind (or the rooster) understanding . . ."

While dressing, one recites, ". . . who clothes the naked."

When resting one's hands on one's eyes, one recites, ". . . who opens the eyes of the blind."

When sitting, one recites, ". . . who releases the bound."

When standing, one recites, ". . . who raised those who are bowed down."

When putting one's feet on the ground, one recites, ". . . who spreads the earth over the water."

When putting on shoes, one recites, ". . . who has provided for all my needs."

When walking, one recites, ". . . who prepares the steps of a person."

When putting on a belt, one recites, ". . . who girds Israel with might."

When putting on a hat, one recites, ". . . who crowns Israel with glory."

When washing the face, one recites, ". . . who removes sleep from my eyes . . ."

(Note: Reuven Kimelman has written an interesting article titled "The Blessings of Prayerobics" (*B'nai Brith Jewish Monthly Magazine*, February 1986) in which he presents some teaching techniques for using various motions during the morning blessings.)

Baruch She'amar

Blessed is He Who spoke, and the world came into being. . . .

Background

Rabbinic commentators have recorded an ancient tradition that this prayer was transcribed by the men of the Great Assembly approximately 2,400 years ago from a script that fell from heaven. The prayer contains eighty-seven words, equal to the numerical equivalent of *paz*, the Hebrew word for "gold." This alludes to the verse in Song of Songs 5:11 that God's opening words are like the finest gold. The prayer *Baruch She'amar* is introduced with a blessing, and is considered the introductory prayer for this new part of the preliminary service that deals with the themes of God's revelation in nature and history.

Concepts

There are seven aspects of God for which we are to praise Him. All of these aspects are mentioned in this prayer, as follows:

1. God spoke, and the world came into being.

2. God speaks and does, decrees and fulfills.

3. God is merciful on Earth.

4. God gives a good reward to those who fear Him.

5. God is eternal.

6. God redeems and rescues people.

7. Blessed is God's name.

Actions

Kabbalists have taught that one should hold one's two front *tzizit* during this prayer and kiss them upon concluding it. This signifies, mystically, that *Baruch She'amar* has an effect on the higher regions of the universe.

Ashrei

Happy are they who dwell in Your house. . . .

Background

The Talmud (*Berachot* 4a) teaches that the rabbis guaranteed a place in the World-to-Come to any person who recited *Ashrei* three times a day. This is because it contains the verse, "You open Your hand and satisfy all living things with favor." God is recognized as the ultimate source in the maintenance of all life. *Ashrei's* prominence among the psalms is also reflected in the Jewish legal ruling that if a person arrives late at services and has time to receive only a single psalm before continuing to pray with the congregation, that the psalm ought to be *Ashrei*.

Beginning with the Hebrew word *aromeimcha*, the initials of the respective verses of *Ashrei* follow the order of the Hebrew alphabet. This literary style is called an alphabetical acrostic, which makes *Ashrei* easier to memorize.

Concepts

1. People are happy when they are close to God.

2. God cares about the oppressed and the poor.

3. God rewards good people and punishes evil ones.

Psalm 150

Halleluyah. Praise God in His sanctuary, in His heaven; for His power praise Him.

Background

In ancient times, musical instruments were played at worship services in the Temple. When the Second Temple was destroyed by the Romans in 70 c.e., the use of instruments ceased, as a sign of mourning for its destruction. (Today, Reform congregations, and some Conservative and Reconstructionist ones, have restored the use of limited music on the Sabbath.)

The Hebrew word *halleluyah* literally means "praise God." It appears in various forms thirteen times in this psalm. Some rabbinic commentators have stated that these thirteen occurrences are symbolic of the thirteen attributes of God revealed in Exodus 34:6–7.

Concepts

There are a variety of ways in which a person can offer praise to God, including dance, song, and the use of musical instruments.

The Song at the Sea

Then Moses and the children of Israel sang this song to God. . . .

Background

Known in Hebrew as *Shirat ha-Yam*, or "The Song at the Sea," this is the victory song that Moses and the Israelites sang after leaving Egypt and crossing the Red Sea (Exodus 14:30–15:19). It is also called *Az Yashir* after its first two Hebrew words, "Then sang . . . ." The song is an amalgamation of biblical verses that include Exodus 15:1–18, Psalms 22:29, Obadiah 1:21, and Zechariah 14:9.

In Temple times, this song, in conjunction with the *Mincha* sacrificial offering, was chanted every Sabbath afternoon by the Levites. After the destruction of the Temple, the song was introduced into the daily morning liturgy. The *Zohar*, the book of Jewish mysticism, states that the person who sings this song with proper intent will merit to sing the praises of future miracles.

Concepts

1. God is a Deliverer and a Savior.

2. God is unique, awesome in power.

3. The miracle of the Israelites crossing the Red Sea clearly demonstrates God's might and His caring relationship with the Jewish people.

4. This prayer is an affirmation of the belief in God's all-important role in human history.

Yishtabach

May Your Name be praised forever.

Background

This prayer officially ends the preliminary section of the morning service. The theme of "fifteen" is repeated twice in this prayer: There are fifteen expressions of praise in the first paragraph, and after the last *Baruch ata Adonai* there are fifteen words. Some commentators say that the number alludes to the fifteen Songs of Ascent (i.e., Psalms 120–134). Also, fifteen is the numerical value of God's name *Yah*.

Tradition ascribes the authorship of this prayer to someone named Shlomo (Solomon). This is because the first letters of the Hebrew words *Shimcha la'ad malkeynu ha-El* in the prayer's first line spell out "Shlomo."

Concepts

1. God's power and might are deserving of our praise and adoration.

2. One must continually praise God.

Barechu

Blessed is God who is to be praised.

Background

Many years ago, the prayers of the preliminary service were said in the privacy of one's home, and the communal morning prayer service began with the Shema and its accompanying blessing. The prayer leader would announce the start of the communal service by calling the congregation to worship. This he did by reciting the words of *Barechu*: *Barechu et Adonai ha-mevorach* ("Blessed is God who is to be praised"). The congregation would respond by saying: *Baruch Adonai ha-mevorach le-olam va'ed* ("Praise God, Source of blessing, forever").

The opening words of the blessing after *Barechu* (called the *yotzer*) have their source in Isaiah 45:7: "Who creates light and darkness, who makes peace and creates evil; I am the God who does all of this." In the blessing in the prayerbook, however, the biblical words "who creates evil" (*u'voray ra*) were changed to "who creates all things" (*u'voray et hakol*).

Some say that this blessing is a polemic against Zoroastrian dualism, which held that there were separate gods of good and evil.

This prayer requires a quorum (*minyan*) of ten persons in order for it to be recited aloud by the reader.

Concepts

1. God is praised for being the Source of all blessings.

2. In the blessing after *Barechu*, we praise God for restoring light to the Earth each morning.

Prayer Motions

The prayer leader bows slightly from the waist when reciting *Barechu*. The congregation does likewise when responding, as a sign of humility to God.

Abavab Rabbah

Deep is your love for us, O Lord our God. . . .

Background

This prayer was probably composed in the time of the Temple. In this prayer, which is the second blessing before the Shema, we thank God for light of Torah and pray that God will grant us the wisdom to understand the Torah properly. The prayer also recalls God's unending love to our ancestors in entrusting His sacred teachings to them.

Concepts

1. God is both a Father and a King. This means that we can feel a close kinship to God, who acts in His aspect as our Parent, while at the same time remaining respectful of the more distant aspect of God, who is also portrayed as a Sovereign Ruler.

2. God chose Israel to be His special people.

3. Israel reciprocates and shows God its love for Him by following His *mitzvot*.

4. Studying the Torah is an important religious obligation.

Prayer Motions

When one reaches the end of the prayer and begins to recite the words *vehaviyanu leshalom* ("bring us safely from the ends of the earth"), the custom is to gather the four corners of one's *tallit*, symbolic of the ingathering of the Jewish people from the four corners of the world.

The Shema

Hear O Israel, the Lord is our God, the Lord is One.

Background

The Shema prayer was publicly recited in the ancient Temple during the service following the recitation of the Ten Commandments. The rabbis included it in both the morning and evening services of the synagogue. The Shema is made up of three biblical paragraphs: Deuteronomy 6:5–9, Deuteronomy 11:13–21, and Numbers 15:37–41. The two paragraphs from Deuteronomy are written on a little scroll that is put into the *mezuzah*, which is placed upon the doorposts of Jewish homes. They are also written on small scrolls that are placed in the *tefillin* that are bound on one's arm and on one's head.

The Shema has become the watchword of the Jewish people. It is one of the first prayers that a young child learns, and it is traditionally said as the last prayer before one dies. Its first six words are recited during the *Kedushah* prayer in the *Amidah*, during the prayer service for taking out the Torah scroll, and at the end of every Yom Kippur service before the final blast of the *shofar*. It is the Torah's classic statement of monotheism (belief in one God).

The last Hebrew letter of the word Shema and the last Hebrew letter of the word *echad* ("one") often appear enlarged in various prayerbooks. These two large letters form the Hebrew word *ayd* ("witness"). Thus every Jew, by pronouncing the Shema, becomes one of God's witnesses, testifying to God's Unity in the world.

Concepts

Paragraph One (Deuteronomy 6:5–9)

1. It is a *mitzvah* to love God with all of one's heart and soul.

2. It is a *mitzvah* to teach one's own children Torah.

3. It is a *mitzvah* to wear *tefillin*.

4. It is a *mitzvah* to affix *mezuzot* to the doorposts of one's home.

Paragraph Two (Deuteronomy 11:13–21)

1. This involves the theology of reward and punishment. If the Jews follow God's ways, they will be rewarded with abundant rain, enabling their crops to grow. If they turn aside to worship other gods, they will be punished by a drought. In the predominantly agricultural society of ancient Israel, lack of water represented ultimate doom.

2. The *mitzvot* of both wearing *tefillin* and affixing *mezuzot* to the doorposts is repeated in this paragraph.

Paragraph Three (Numbers 15:37–41)

1. It is a *mitzvah* to wear *tzitzit* (fringes) on the corners of one's garment. This refers to the *tallit* (prayer shawl).

2. Israel is warned to be a holy people and to always

remember the miraculous redemption from Egyptian bondage.

Prayer Motions

1. The custom is to cover one's eyes when reciting the opening line of the Shema: "Hear O Israel, the Lord is our God, the Lord is One." This keeps the worshipper away from distraction and allows him or her to concentrate on God's Oneness.

2. There is a custom, when saying the words, "and they shall be for frontlets between your eyes," to kiss the head *tefillin* by kissing one's fingers and touching them to the box of the head *tefillin*.

3. It is customary to gather the four fringes of one's prayer shawl and kiss them three times, once each time that the word *tzitzit* (fringe) is mentioned in the third paragraph of the Shema. In this way, the worshipper symbolically embraces God's command-ments.

Special Recitation Customs

1. The second line of the Shema, *Baruch shem kavod malchuto le'olam va'ed* ("Blessed is the Name of His glorious kingdom forever"), is recited silently, except during the High Holy Days (with the theme of God as the Sovereign of sovereigns), when it is chanted aloud for added emphasis. One reason given in the Midrash (Deuteronomy Rabbah 2:36) for its silent rendering is that Moses heard this prayer from the

angels, and taught it to Israel. People dare not to say it aloud, because people are sinful and, thus, unworthy of uttering an angelic formula. This response, first used in the Temple during the Yom Kippur service, was later made the accompaniment of the opening verse of the Shema.

2. The three final words at the end of the Shema, *Adonai Eloheichem emet* ("I am the Lord your God, true . . .") are repeated aloud by the reader so that the number of words in the Shema—which actually has only 245 words—now totals 248, corresponding to the 248 limbs of the human body, all of which should praise God.

Mi Kamocha

Who is like You, O God, among the mighty . . . .

Background

The words of this prayer (Exodus 15:11) are part of The Song at the Sea, which the children of Israel sang when they crossed the Red Sea after leaving Egypt. The whole song can be found in Exodus 15.

Concepts

1. There is none that can compare to God.

2. God is Holy and worthy of praise because He can perform miracles.

3. This prayer concludes with the blessing that praises God as Redeemer of Israel.

Special Recitation Customs

The last line of *Mi Kamocha*, which constitutes the blessing *Baruch ata Adonai Ga'al Yisrael* ("Blessed are You, O Lord, Redeemer of Israel") is chanted by the reader in a low tone. This is done in a symbolic gesture not to interrupt the redemption from the *Amidah* prayer that immediately follows.

Amidah

Background

The *Amidah* (i.e., the standing prayer), also known as the *Shemoneh Esrei* ("Eighteen"), is the central element of the three daily services. It is spoken of in the Talmud as *Hatefillah*, the prayer par excellence, on account of its importance and its antiquity. According to tradition, it was composed by members of the Great Assembly in the early period of the Second Temple.

Originally, the *Shemoneh Esrei* consisted of eighteen blessings. In its present form, however, it contains nineteen blessings. The addition of the paragraph concerning the slanderers and enemies of the Jewish people was made toward the end of the first century c.e., at the direction of Rabban Gamaliel II, head of the Sanhedrin (High Court) at Yavneh.

The Talmud offers a variety of reasons for the number eighteen. It corresponds to the eighteen times God is mentioned in Psalm 29, as well as in the Shema. Also, the three Patriarchs of the Jewish people, Abraham, Isaac, and Jacob, are mentioned together eighteen times in the Torah. The number eighteen is also said to correspond to the essential eighteen vertebrae of the human spinal column (*Berachot* 28b).

Today this prayer is generally referred to as the *Amidah*, so named because it is recited in a standing position. The name *Amidah* accurately describes this prayer for Sabbaths and Festivals, when it consists of seven blessings only. In Orthodox synagogues and in some Conservative synagogues, the *Amidah* of *Shacharit* and *Mincha* is first recited in an undertone by each person in the congregation, and then aloud by the reader on behalf of the congregation. This repetition of the *Amidah* is for the benefit of those who cannot read the *Amidah* for themselves. The *Amidah* is never repeated aloud by the reader during the *Ma'ariv*. This is because the rabbis held that the evening *Amidah* was optional, not obligatory.

On the Sabbath and Festivals, the first three and the last three blessings of the *Amidah* are the same. The thirteen petitions of the weekday *Amidah* are eliminated on the grounds that no personal requests may be made on the Sabbath or Festivals.

The middle paragraphs of the weekday *Amidah* contain petitions for the fulfillment of needs, including wisdom, repentance, healing, prosperity, and restoration of justice, to name a few.

The *Amidah*, like *Barechu*, requires a quorum of ten in order for it to be recited aloud by the reader.

Concepts

Here are the basic themes of each of the nineteen blessings of the weekday Amidah.

1. *Avot* (Ancestors): God is the God of our ancestors;

He was their Protector, and He continues to be our Protector.

2. *Gevurot* (Power): God's power in nature is great, and extends to giving life to the dead.

3. *Kedushah* (Sanctification): God is unique and is a holy God.

4. *Da'at* (Knowledge): We petition God in this fourth blessing for knowledge and understanding.

5. *Teshuvah* (Repentance): We ask God to accept our repentance.

6. *Selicha* (Forgiveness): We ask God to grant us forgiveness.

7. *Ge'ulah* (Redemption): We praise God for redeeming the Israelites.

8. *Refu'ah* (Healing): We praise God for healing our people, and ask that we be healed.

9. *Birkat HaShanim* (Blessing the Years): We praise God for satisfying us with many years of blessing.

10. *Kibbutz Galuyot* (Ingathering of the Exiles): We praise God for gathering the dispersed.

11. *Tzedakah U'Mishpat* (Justice and Mercy): We petition God to sustain us with justice and mercy.

12. *Malshinim* (Maligners): We ask God to humble the arrogant and frustrate the hopes of those who malign us.

13. *Tzaddikim* (Righteous Ones): We ask God to sustain righteous people.

14. *Yerushalayim* (Jerusalem): We ask God to rebuild Jerusalem.

15. *Dovid* (David): We ask God to bring to flower the shoot of David and ensure our deliverance.

16. *Shome'ah Tefillah* (Hears Our Prayers): We petition God to listen to our prayers.

17. *Avodah* (Worship): We ask God to accept our prayers.

18. *Hoda'ah* (Thanksgiving): We thank God for the daily miracles of life, and acknowledge their Source.

19. *Shalom* (Peace): We praise God and pray for peace in the world.

Prayer Motions

1. Before beginning the *Amidah*, the custom is to take three steps backward and then three steps forward while saying the introductory words, *Adonai sifatai tiftach ufi yaggid tehillatecha* ("Open my mouth and my lips will proclaim Your praise"). This is a symbolic way of bowing before God the Sovereign.

2. At the end of the *Amidah*, it is customary to take three steps backward on the words *Oseh shalom bimromav* ("May He who brings peace to the heavens") and then bend left at the waist. On the words *hu ya'aseh shalom* ("He will grant peace"), it is customary to bend right at the waist. At the words *aleynu ve'al kol yisrael* ("for us and all of Israel"), it is customary to bend forward at the waist. This is the reverse of the approach to God at the beginning of the *Amidah*, for one is now taking leave of God.

3. There are four times when one customarily bows during the *Amidah*. Bowing in these places is a sign of humility toward God, the Sovereign One. They include:

   a. At the beginning of the *Amidah*, on the words *Baruch ata Adonai Elohaynu vaylohay avotaynu* ("Blessed is the Lord, the God of our ancestors").

   b. On the words *Baruch ata Adonai magen Avraham* ("Blessed is the Lord, Shield of Abraham").

   c. On the words *Modim anachnu lach* ("We gratefully thank You"), a phrase from 1 Chronicles 29:13.

   d. On the words *Baruch ata Adonai hatov shimcha ulecha na'eh lehodot* ("Blessed are You, O Lord, Your Name is the beneficent One, to Whom all praise is due").

4. On the words *Kadosh, kadosh, kadosh* ("Holy, holy, holy") in the *Kedushah*, the custom is to rise to one's tiptoes, thus symbolically reaching toward heaven.

5. The *Amidah* is said while standing with feet touching. Standing at attention when praying is a mark of respect. A biblical basis for this requirement is found in Ezekiel 1:7: "And their feet were as a straight foot." This is interpreted in Tractate *Berachot* 10b to mean that the feet of the angels in Ezekiel's vision appeared as one foot. When a person stands to speak to God, that person ought to assume the position of the ministering angels.

Elohai Netzor

O God, guard my lips from speaking evil . . . .

Background

Several different rabbis wrote closing prayers to the *Amidah*. This one, called *Elohai Netzor*, was composed by Mar bar Ravina, a fourteenth-century scholar. Originally it was said as a private meditation, asking God to guard our tongue from speaking evil. The prayer is unusual in structure in that it was written in the first person, whereas most communal prayers are written in plural form.

Concepts

1. A person's words are capable of perpetrating evil.

2. Humility and modesty are Jewish virtues.

3. God will answer our prayers because He is an all-powerful and compassionate God.

4. God will bring peace to the world.

Tachanun

He, the merciful One, grants atonement from sin and does not destroy.

Background

Jewish tradition provides for optional and personal prayer as well as obligatory prayer. The prayer known as *Tachanun* (Supplications) includes supplications and confession of one's sins. It affords the worshipper an opportunity to offer personal prayers, as well as various supplications and confessions from traditional sources. It is recited on weekdays after the *Amidah*, and is often referred to as *nefilat apayim* ("falling on the face") because in early talmudic times it was customary to recite it while prostrating oneself. This custom derived from Moses, who "lay prostrate before God" [Deuteronomy 9:18], and Joshua, who fell to the earth upon his face before the Ark of God (Joshua 7:6). Nowadays, the custom is to recite *Tachanun* while sitting and resting one's head on one's arm. On Mondays and Thursdays, days on which the Torah is read, the "longer" *Tachanun*, which contains heartrending supplications giving voice to the sufferings of the Jewish people, is said.

Concepts

1. God is a forgiving God who is compassionate and gracious.
2. God will answer our call and treat us with kindness because of His mercy.

Prayer Motions

It is customary to recite *Tanchanun* while seated and resting one's head on one's arm. This is the posture of one who asks forgiveness for his or her sins.

Kedushah d'Sidra

And a redeemer shall come . . . .

Background

This prayer, also known as *Uva l'tziyon,* is generally known as *Kedushah d'Sidra* (Sanctification of the Torah Portion) because its first two verses are taken from Isaiah 59:20–21. At one time, the recitation of this prayer followed the reading of a Sidra, or portion of the Prophets, which would customarily be read at the end of daily services. The two opening verses of this prayer from the prophetic book of Isaiah reflect a hint of this ancient practice.

It is assumed that the motivation for introducing this prayer at the end of the worship service was to allow those latecomers who missed *Kedushah* in the *Amidah* to have an opportunity to say a prayer with a similar theme.

Concepts

1. A redeemer will be brought by God to save the world.

2. God's righteousness will last forever.

3. Blessed is the person who trusts in God.

Kaddish

Magnified and sanctified be the Name of God . . . .

Background

Originally, the Kaddish (Sanctification) prayer was used as a short prayer at the close of sermons that were delivered in Aramaic, the language spoken by the Jewish people for approximately one thousand years after the Babylonian captivity. Kaddish was recited in Aramaic, the tongue in which the religious discourses were held. At a later period, Kaddish was introduced into the liturgy to mark the conclusion of sections of the service, as well as the end of both biblical and talmudic readings recited in public.

Since the merit of studying the Torah was given high priority, the idea arose that the living might, through Torah study, benefit the remembrance of the deceased. Hence, such study was assigned to mourners. A Talmud study or a religious discourse was conducted for them, which was concluded by the reader's recitation of the Kaddish prayer. Gradually, Kaddish became an indirect prayer for the deceased.

There are several different forms of the Kaddish prayer, including *Chatzi* Kaddish (Half Kaddish), Kaddish *Shalem* (Full Kaddish), Kaddish *Yatom* (Orphan's or Mourner's Kaddish), Kaddish *d'Rabbanan* (Rabbi's or Scholar's Kaddish), and *Kaddish d'Itchaddata* (Kaddish of Renewal, or Burial Kaddish).

The opening Hebrew of all of these Kaddish prayers, *Yitgadal veyitkadash* ("Magnified and sanctified [is God's Name]") is said to have been inspired by the prophet Ezekiel's vision of a time when God will become great and hallowed in the eyes of all of the nations (Ezekiel 38:23). Basically, all the forms of Kaddish praise God and God's Name, and yearn for the speedy establishment of God's kingdom on earth. Kaddish, like *Barechu* and the *Amidah*, requires a *minyan* of ten in order to be recited aloud.

The congregational Hebrew response to the Kaddish is *Yehai shemai rabbah mevorach le-olam u-le'almay almaya* ("May God be praised throughout all time"). This line was added to the Kaddish prayer in approximately the eighth century.

The earliest version of Kaddish, called Half Kaddish, dates back to the period of the Second Temple. The Rabbi's Kaddish was traditionally recited when the rabbis finished their lecture-sermons on Sabbath afternoons, and includes a special prayer for rabbis, scholars, and their disciples.

The Full Kaddish contains a special paragraph that begins with the Hebrew word *Titkabel* ("May it be accepted"), in which it asks that God accept all of one's prayers.

The first mention of the custom that mourners say Kaddish at the end of every worship service is found in *Ohr Zarua*, a thirteenth-century work by one of the early rabbinic authorities. The Mourner's Kaddish, which makes no direct reference to death, became a means whereby a bereaved person could express his or her acceptance of God's divine Judgment.

Finally, the Burial Kaddish is recited by traditional mourners at the cemetery immediately following the burial. Its first paragraph has a reference to the revival of the dead and giving the dead eternal life.

Concepts

1. God's name is holy and great.

2. God's sovereignty will be accepted by all.

3. God will bring peace to the world.

4. God will resurrect the dead (Burial Kaddish).

Aleynu

It is incumbent upon us to praise God . . .

Background

The prayer known as *Aleynu*, which proclaims God as Sovereign over a united humanity, has been recited as the closing prayer of the three daily services since the thirteenth century. According to an ancient tradition, Joshua, the successor to Moses, composed it when he entered the Promised Land. It is generally held, however, that it was first introduced by Rav, founder of the Sura Academy (third century C.E.) as an introduction to the *Malchuyot* (Kingship) section recited as part of the *Musaf* service for Rosh Hashanah.

One of the earliest forms of the *Aleynu* prayer (which still appears in some traditional payerbooks) contains the statement: *Shehem mishtachavim · lehevel va'rik u'mitpalelim l'el lo yoshiah* ("They bow down to vanity and emptiness, and pray to a God that will not save"). This was based upon two biblical verses (Isaiah 30:7 and 45:20). In the Middle Ages, Christian authorities censored this line because they felt that it demeaned Jesus. (Note: They arrived at this conclusion because the phrase "emptiness" [in Hebrew, *varik*] had the same numerical value in *gematria* as the word *Yeshua* [Hebrew for "Jesus"].)

Concepts

1. In the first paragraph of *Aleynu*, we praise God for creating the universe and for choosing the Jews to be God's special people.

2. In the second paragraph of the Shema, a more universalistic theme is prevalent. It concludes with a verse from the prophet Zechariah (14:9), who envisions a time in the future when all people will acknowledge that God is One and God's Name is One.

Actions

It is customary to bend the knees and bow when reciting *Va'anachnu korim u'mishtachavim u'modim* ("We bend the knee, bow, worship, and give thanks").

Psalms for the Day

Background

During the ancient Temple service, the Levites would sing a special psalm for each day of the week. Today, we continue this tradition by reciting a psalm for each day at the conclusion of the morning service. Each psalm is introduced with the phrase, "Today is the first [second, third, etc.] day" as a symbolic countdown to the Sabbath, which comes at the end of each week. Each psalm of the day, in its own way, reflects a theme related to the Creation of the world.

Concepts

Psalm for Sunday (Psalm 24): God created heaven and earth. The person who has a clean heart and mind will receive God's blessing.

Psalm for Monday (Psalm 48): God's Presence appears on earth, and God will continue to guide people forever.

Psalm for Tuesday (Psalm 82): People must champion the causes of the weak and downtrodden; otherwise, God will make the very foundation of the earth tremble.

Psalm for Wednesday (Psalm 94): God knows the schemes of evil and will never abandon His nation.

Psalm for Thursday (Psalm 81): God has always rescued His people in time of distress, and He will continue to do so. People must listen to God and walk in His ways.

Psalm for Friday (Psalm 93): God has set the world on an unshakable foundation. Even though the waters rage, the earth will continue to stand firm.

Psalm for *Shabbat* (Psalm 92): The righteous will continue to flourish, while the evil are doomed.

Adon Olam

Master of the universe, who reigned eternal before the birth of every living thing.

Background

Adon Olam is a hymn that has been attributed to various medieval poets—mainly to Solomon ibn Gabirol, who lived in Spain during the eleventh century. In his famous philosophical poem *Keter Malchut* ("Royal Crown"), ibn Gabirol addresses God in themes similar to that of *Adon Olam*.

Several rabbinic authorities have suggested that *Adon Olam* was originally meant as a night prayer, since it concludes with: "I entrust my spirit into His hand when I sleep . . . ."

There are many different musical settings and melodies for *Adon Olam*.

Concepts

1. God is eternal and sovereign.

2. God is One and has no equal.

3. God redeems and is our refuge. God is always on our side, and when we go to sleep we need not be afraid.

Sabbath and Festival Prayer Synopsis

The following is a cross-section of the more important and well-known prayers of the Sabbath and Festival services.

SABBATH EVENING

Psalms 95 to 99

Background

The conception of the Sabbath as a bride and queen, and the custom of welcoming her, have interesting historical roots. The Talmud (*Shabbat* 119a) describes how the rabbis would dress in white on Friday evening to greet the Sabbath Queen. It became customary for Psalms 95 to 99 to be recited at this time by the mystics, particularly

Moses Cordovero, who lived in the holy city of Safed in northern Israel. The psalms were recited prior to the *Ma'ariv* service, which began with *Barechu*. Some commentators have said that the six psalms symbolize the six working days of the week, and that each one praises God for the glory of His creations. Others have said that the initial Hebrew letters of each of these six psalms have the numerical value of 430, which is the numerical value of the word *nefesh* (meaning "soul").

Concepts

1. We thank God for His creations (Psalms 95–99, 29).

2. All of the world's nations are called upon to acknowledge God's power (Psalm 96).

3. God is supreme over all of the earth, and God's light is stored for righteous people (Psalm 97).

4. All of the world, including natural phenomena (river, mountains), praise God (Psalm 98).

5. God is Sovereign and maintains justice throughout the world (Psalm 99).

6. God's majesty is felt in the storm, as God's voice shatters trees and makes mountains leap. God ultimately will bestow a blessing of *shalom* ("peace") on all His people.

Lecha Dodi

Come, my Beloved, to greet the bride.

Background

This hymn has been described as one of the finest pieces of liturgical poetry. It was written by Rabbi Solomon Alkabets, a sixteenth-century mystic, and has become universally popular as a hymn welcoming the Sabbath. The name of the author, Shlomo haLevi, is found in the form of an acrostic at the beginnings of the stanzas. Phrases from Judges, Isaiah, Jeremiah, and Psalms are combined into a mosaic forming this hymn. The name *Lecha Dodi* is borrowed from the Song of Songs (7:12), which states: "Come, my beloved, let us go into the field. . . ."

Concepts

1. The first stanza of *Lecha Dodi* recalls the midrashic interpretation of two of the Ten Commandments: "Remember the Sabbath day" (Exodus 20:8) and "Observe the Sabbath" (Deuteronomy 5:12). According to rabbinic legend, God uttered the Hebrew words for "Remember" and "Observe" simultaneously, thus signifying that both observance and remembrance are necessary in order to honor the Sabbath day.

2. The Sabbath is the symbolic ideal of all Creation.

3. Jerusalem will eventually be rebuilt, thus enabling the coming of the Messiah.

Prayer Motions

At the end of the hymn, during the recitation of the last verse, *Bo'ee veshalom* ("Come in peace"), the custom is to turn to the entrance of the sanctuary and bow to the right and the left in a symbolic greeting of the Sabbath bride.

Psalm 92: A Psalm for the Sabbath Day

A Song of Shabbat. It is good to acclaim God, to sing Your praise . . . .

Background

This is the only psalm with a heading that connects the psalm with the Sabbath day itself. In the ancient Temple, it was chanted by the Levites each Sabbath. The World-to-Come, in rabbinic thought, is considered as being one unending Sabbath. This may be the true relationship between this psalm and the Sabbath itself.

Concepts

1. It is good to thank God.

2. Eventually, all wicked people will be utterly destroyed.

3. The righteous will flourish and will continue to bear fruit in their old age.

4. God is upright and has no flaws.

Hashkivaynu

Help us to lie down in peace . . . .

Background

This prayer for peace contains the final blessing after the Shema: ". . . who spreads the tabernacle of peace of us, over all His people Israel, and over Jerusalem." Today, it is often recited by those who find themselves in dangerous situations.

Concepts

1. God has the ability to shield people from enemies and evil forces.

2. God is a gracious and merciful Ruler.

3. We praise God for spreading a tabernacle of peace over the Jews, and especially over Jerusalem.

Veshamru

And the children of Israel will observe the Sabbath and keep it through the generations as an everlasting covenant (Exodus 31:16–17).

Background

This biblical text presents the important connection between the Sabbath and the Jewish people. The Sabbath is the special sign of the eternal covenant that God made with the children of Israel.

Concepts

The Sabbath is a sign of God's eternal covenant with the Jewish people. In order to keep the covenant, Israel must observe the Sabbath.

Magen Avot

God's world was a shield to our ancestors.

Background

This prayer is an abridged form of the *Amidah* for Sabbath evening. It is also known as *me'ayn sheva* ("a form of seven") because it contains the substance of the seven blessings constituting the Sabbath *Amidah*. *Magen Avot* was originally added to the liturgy in order to prolong the service for the convenience of latecomers who may have missed the recitation of the *Amidah*.

Concepts

1. God is a shield to our ancestors.

2. God's word gives life to the dead.

3. God is a holy God.

4. God favored His people to give them rest.

5. We will serve God with fear and awe.

6. We shall give thanks to God's Name.

7. God sanctifies the Sabbath.

Kiddush: **The Blessing over Wine**

Blessed are You, O Lord our God, Ruler of the Universe, who creates the fruit of the vine.

Background

The custom of reciting a blessing over wine in the synagogue arose during talmudic times as a gesture of hospitality for wayfarers who often would eat their meals in the synagogue. Wine is Judaism's most revered beverage, and is often represented metaphorically as the essence of goodness. Psalm 104 (Psalms 104:15) says that "wine cheers God and humans." The origin of kiddush ("sanctification") traces back to the early period of the Second Temple, and is attributed to the men of the Great Assembly who flourished at that time.

Concepts

1. The blessing over wine is recited as a remembrance of God's Creation of the world and the Exodus from Egypt.

2. God showed His love for the Israelites by giving them the Sabbath.

3. God chose the people of Israel and endowed them with holiness.

Yigdal

The living God, magnify and bless . . . .

Background

This hymn was composed by Rabbi Daniel ben Yehudah of Rome, a fourteenth-century poet. It consists of thirteen lines that summarize the Thirteen Principles of Faith formulated by Moses Maimonides in his Mishnah commentary.

Concepts

1. There is a Creator.

2. God's Oneness is absolute.

3. God has no body.

4. God is eternal.

5. God alone may be worshipped.

6. The prophets are true.

7. Moses is the greatest of all the prophets.

8. The entire Torah was Divinely given to Moses.

9. The Torah is immutable.

10. God knows all of the thoughts of human beings.

11. God rewards and punishes.

12. The Messiah will come.

13. God will resurrect the dead.

SABBATH AND FESTIVAL MORNINGS

El Adon

God is Master over all of His works.

Background

This alphabetical but unrhymed hymn is from the medieval period. It has been attributed to the *Yorde Merkavah*, the eighth-century mystics. Basically, this prayer is a praise of God, who created the sun, moon, and stars. Having spoken of the sun and the moon, the poet alludes to the planets Saturn, Venus, Mercury, Jupiter, and Mars by means of the first letters of the words of the last of the six stanzas, which reads: *Shevach notnim lo kol tzva marom.* The Hebrew names of the mentioned planets are *Ma'adim, Tzedek, Kochav, Noga,* and *Shabbtai.*

Concepts

1. God created good lights that radiate brilliance.
2. All heavenly bodies praise God.

Eyn Keloheynu

None compares to our God . . . .

Background

This prayer is sung at the end of the Sabbath and Festival morning service. Sephardic Jews also recite it on weekdays. Its first three stanzas form the acrostic "Amen," a prayer response meaning "so be it."

Concepts

1. God is One and unique.

2. We praise God and submit to His will.

3. We acknowledge God as Ruler and Sovereign.

Hallel: Psalms of Praise

Background

Hallel (psalms of praise), recited on the Festivals, consists of Psalms 113 to 118. It is also called the *Hallel Mitzri* ("Egyptian *Hallel*") because Psalm 114 refers to the Exodus from Egypt and begins with the phrase, "When Israel went out of Egypt." On Purim, the reading of the *Megillah* takes the place of *Hallel*. *Hallel* also is not recited on Rosh Hashanah and Yom Kippur, since these holidays are not a time of jubilation.

To celebrate Rosh Chodesh, a minor Festival marking the start of a new month, an abridged *Hallel* called *Chatzi Hallel* ("Half Hallel") is recited. In the *Half Hallel*, the first eleven verses of Psalms 115 and 116 are omitted. *Half Hallel* is also recited on the last six days of Passover, because it is said that God restrained the angels from singing His praise upon seeing the Egyptians drowning in the Red Sea on the seventh day of Passover.

Concepts

1. God lifts the poor out of the dust and God's glory extends beyond the heavens (Psalm 113).

2. The Jews are God's holy people. Even the earth trembles at God's Presence (Psalm 114).

3. Idols are useless, whereas God can do whatever He wishes (Psalm 115).

4. God is gracious and compassionate. God delivers from death (Psalm 116).

5. God's love has overwhelmed the people; therefore, God should be praised (Psalm 117).

6. It is better to depend on God than to trust in mortals. God's love endures forever (Psalm 118).

HIGH-HOLIDAY PRAYERS

Kol Nidray:

This prayer, written in Aramaic, is the ancient formula recited at the start of the Day of Atonement for the dispensation of one's vows. *Kol Nidray* ("all vows") refers to vows assumed by an individual for himself or herself alone, with no other people or their interests involved.

According to the *Machzor Vitry*—composed by Rabbi Simcha Vitry, a disciple of the medieval commentator Rashi—the reader chants *Kol Nidray* very softly the first time, like one who hesitates to enter the king's palace and fears to come near him with a request for a favor; the second time he chants somewhat louder; the third time he raises his voice louder still, like one accustomed to being a member of the king's court. *Kol Nidray* is chanted before sundown because, according to Jewish law, dispensation of vows may not be granted on Sabbaths or Holy Days.

Although the *Kol Nidray* prayer existed in the time of Rav Amram, it was changed to the future tense by Rabbi Jacob Tam in the Middle Ages so that it applied to vows about to be contracted "between this Yom Kippur and the next Yom Kippur." Support for this change is found in the talmudic statement (*Nedarim* 23b): "Whoever desires that none of his vows made during the year shall be valid, let him declare at the beginning of the year: 'May all the vows which I am likely to make in the future be annulled.'" This was in consideration of the weaknesses of human nature and the tragic results of promises that are too hastily made.

Concepts

1. Our words must be taken seriously.

2. We ask to be released from vows to God that were unkept because of circumstances beyond our control.

The Confessional (*Ashamnu*)

We have trespassed, we have dealt treacherously. . . .

Background

Said repeatedly on Yom Kippur, the Confessional, sometimes called *Ashamnu* ("We have sinned"), developed over many centuries. The prayer is an alphabetical acrostic in which all letters of the Hebrew alphabet are used in succession. *Ashamnu* is rendered in the plural to stress the solidarity of the Jewish community. A longer version of this prayer, *Al Chayt* ("For the sin"), developed after the Talmud was written.

Concepts

We accept communal responsibility for the multitude of mistakes that the Jewish community as a whole made during the past year. Wrongs committed with the tongue are stressed.

Prayer Motions

It is customary to beat one's breast with the right hand upon reciting each transgression in both of the confessionals. This is symbolic of our sincere repentance.

Unetaneh Tokef

Let us describe the mighty holiness of this day, for it is one of awe and anxiety.

Background

This prayer poem figures prominently in the *Musaf* service for the High Holy Days. Its authorship is attributed to Rabbi Amnon of Mayence, a legendary martyr at the time of the Crusades, immediately preceding his demise. According to some, three days after his death, Rabbi Amnon appeared to Rabbi Kalonymus ben

Meshullam—one of the eminent *payyetanim* in eleventh-century Germany, taught him the prayer, and asked him to make it part of the prayer service.

The prayer describes, in exalted language, the heavenly procedure on the Day of Judgment, in which it was decreed "who shall live and who shall die, who by fire and who by water . . . ."

The conclusion of the prayer affirms that "prayer, charity, and repentance avert the evil decree."

Concepts

1. God is the Shepherd of His flock, the Israelites, whom He supports.

2. Life is uncertain, and one will encounter difficulties.

3. True repentance involves doing deeds of kindness and praying with proper intention.

The Sounding of the *Shofar*

The sounding of the *shofar* was originally mandated for all holidays and the New Moon. Since the destruction of the Temple, the *shofar* (ram's horn) is sounded only on the High Holy Days and on each morning during the month of Elul in preparation for the Days of Awe.

In the Ashkenazic ritual, Psalm 47 (with its reference to God manifesting Himself with the sounding of the *shofar*) precedes the shofar-blowing.

The sounds produced by the *shofar* are *tekiah* (one long sound), *shevarim* (three broken notes), and *teruah* (nine short staccato notes).

Some have called the sounding of the *shofar* a prayer without words. Its shrill sounds are intended to awaken in the worshipper the desire to repent.

Concepts

1. We proclaim God's sovereignty when we sound the *shofar*.

2. The *shofar* is intended to motivate worshippers to repent, reminding them of the Day of Judgment.

3. Saadia Gaon, the tenth-century philosopher, offered the following reasons for blowing the *shofar*:

   a. It proclaims the sovereignty of God.

   b. It warns people to change their lives.

   c. It reminds people of the revelation at Mount Sinai, when the *shofar* was heard.

   d. It brings to mind the prophetic warnings.

   e. It is reminiscent of the battle alarm in Judea.

   f. It reminds us of Abraham's attempted sacrifice of his son Isaac.

   g. It inspires the heart with awe and reverence.

   h. It reminds us of the Day of Judgment.

   i. It fills us with hope for the final restoration of the people of Israel.

   j. It is identified with the time of the resurrection of the dead.

The Rosh Hashanah Additional (*Musaf*) Service

Background

The *Musaf* service for the New Year has nine blessings instead of the seven usually recited on Festivals. The first three and the last three are the same. The middle three blessings are:

Malchuyot (Kingship verses)
Zichronot (Remembrance verses)
Shofarot (Proclamation verses)

Each of these three sections contains ten biblical verses that relate to God's sovereignty; the concept of God remembering His people; and verses that relate to the sounding of the ram's horn. Three verses for each section are from the Five Books of Moses, three are from the Book of Writings, and three are from the Books of the Prophets. One additional verse in each section is derived from the Five Books of Moses. Following each section of verses, the *shofar* is sounded.

Concepts

1. The *Malchuyot* verses proclaim God as the Sovereign of sovereigns, before Whom an entire people stand in judgment.

2. The *Zichronot* verses are a reminder that God is a God of justice Who rewards and punishes people according to their actions.

3. The *Shofarot* verses recall God's miraculous revelation at Mount Sinai.

Avinu Malkeynu

Our Father, our Sovereign One, we have sinned before You.

Background

This prayer consists of a series of invocations and supplications recited in the synagogue services during the ten-day period of the High Holy Days and on fasts (except for the Ninth of Av). It is not recited on the Sabbath because its petitionary nature is unsuitable for the joyousness of the Sabbath. It is mentioned in *Taanit* 25b as the improvised prayer of Rabbi Akiba on the occasion of a drought.

The phrase *Avinu Malkeynu* ("Our Father, our Sovereign One") is borrowed from Isaiah 33:22, 63:16, and 64:7. The prayer reflects the frequent persecutions that have given rise to outcries such as "Our Father, our Sovereign One," "Rid us of every oppressor," and so forth.

Concepts

1. We can relate to God as a Parent with all of a parent's warmth. We also can relate to God as the Sovereign One, awesome, distant, and unknowable.

2. We petition God to fulfill a variety of requests, including blessings, health, acceptance of prayers, removal of pestilence, and annulment of evil decrees.

RESPONSES IN PRAYER

There are several important responses that worshippers make during prayer service. The most famous one is the Hebrew word *amen,* which has entered almost every language in the world. In the Bible it is used as a term of affirmation. For instance, in Deuteronomy 27:16–26, we find a series of pronouncements by the Levites to which the people responded "amen." 1 Chronicles (16:35) clearly portrays that, in the time of King David, the Israelites responded "amen" upon hearing the blessing, "Blessed be the God of Israel from now until all eternity."

During the Second-Temple period, "amen" served as a response to blessings and prayers recited outside the Temple. By pronouncing "amen," the listener associated himself with what had been uttered, thus making it his or her own and showing his or her readiness to conform to it. The Israelites said "amen" to the Ten Commandments that Moses gave them, thus agreeing to follow them and to accept all of the consequences implied.

Rabbinic thinkers have attributed great significance to the word "amen." According to a talmudic statement (*Sanhedrin* 111a), the initial letters of the words *El Melech Ne'eman* ("God is a faithful King") form the word *amen*. The sages regarded the "amen" response as a fulfillment of the biblical verse in Deuteronomy 32:3: "When I proclaim the name of the Lord, give glory to our God." This was interpreted to mean that when the Name of God is blessed, we declare God's greatness by answering "amen." Jewish law has ruled that any person who hears another recite a blessing is required to respond "amen" upon its conclusion (*Code of Jewish Law*, Orach Chayyim 215:2).

This legal ruling was especially important before the advent of the printed prayerbook. Since most people did not know the liturgy by heart and few hand-copied prayerbooks were in existence, listening to the prayer leader and responding "amen" at the appropriate times was their way of fulfilling their obligation. The "amen" response continues to be a meaningful one, especially in services when the *Amidah* prayer is repeated aloud by the prayer leader, requiring the congregational response of "amen" in numerous places.

RULES FOR SAYING "AMEN"

There are several rules to keep in mind regarding the response of "amen." They include the following:

1. One does not respond "amen" to a blessing that one has recited for oneself.

2. "Amen" may be said when hearing a blessing recited by a gentile (*Code of Jewish Law*, Orach Chayyim 215:2).

3. One must not respond "amen" to a blessing made in vain (*Code of Jewish Law*, Orach Chayyim 215:4).

4. When in the midst of praying, one may not be interrupted, and may not stop, in order to say "amen."

5. For educational purposes, one ought to answer "amen" to a blessing recited by a child (*Code of Jewish Law*, Orach Chayyim 215:3).

6. One should not say "amen" in a tone louder than the blessing itself (*Code of Jewish Law*, Orach Chayyim 124:12).

7. One should always pronounce the word "amen" distinctly, without rushing (*Code of Jewish Law*, Orach Chayyim 124:8).

8. One should always answer "amen" after the *entire* blessing has been completed (*Code of Jewish Law*, Orach Chayyim 124:8).

9. One should never answer "amen" to a blessing that one does not actually hear. Such a response is called an "orphaned amen" and is expressly forbidden (*Code of Jewish Law*, Orach Chayyim 124:8).

10. According to some rabbinic authorities, "amen" is not said upon a blessing that is heard on the radio or on television.

NOTABLE "AMEN" QUOTATIONS

Following are some quotations from the Talmud and various *midrashim* related to the "amen" response and its importance in Jewish life.

1. One who answers "amen" is greater than the one who recites the blessing (*Berachot* 53b).

2. Anyone who answers "amen" with all his might, the gates of paradise are opened for him (*Shabbat* 119b).

3. One who answers "amen" in this world will merit to answer "amen" in the World-to-Come (Deuteronomy Rabbah 7:1).

4. Those who belittle the response "amen" go down to *Gehinnom* (*Zohar* 3 285b).

5. When the Jews observe the response of "amen" and concentrate properly, many gates of blessing are opened for them in heaven, and much goodness is found in all the worlds (*Zohar* 3 285b).

OTHER LITURGICAL RESPONSES

Several other liturgical responses permeate the liturgy. Here is a summary of the more important ones.

1. *Baruch hu u'varuch shemo* ("Blessed be He and blessed be His Name"). This is the correct response upon hearing the Name of God (*Adonai*) in the opening part of the blessing (i.e., *Baruch ata Adonai*). However, one does not respond *Baruch hu u'varuch*

shemo to a blessing that is being said with the intent to fulfill the obligation of the listener, such as the blessing on the *shofar*. Responding *Baruch hu u'varuch shemo* to such a blessing is inappropriate, because it is, in a sense, an interruption in the middle of one's blessing.

2. *Baruch Adonai hamevorach l'olam va'ed* ("Blessed be God Who is blessed for all eternity"). This is the liturgical response to the person who is honored with an *aliyah* to the Torah and recites the opening line, *Barechu et Adonai hamevorach* ("Bless the Lord Who is to be praised").

3. *Kein yehi ratzon* ("So may it be"). This is the congregational response to the three verses of the Priestly Benediction, recited by the prayer leader, that begins *Yevarechecha Adonai veyishmerecha* ("May the Lord bless you and watch over you").

4. *Halleluyah* ("Praise the Lord"). This is the congregational response to the so-called "*Halleluyah* psalms"—especially those in the *Hallel* service, many of which end in *Halleluyah*. During Temple times, *halleluyah* was a directive from the presiding functionary to the worshipping congregation in the Temple, and was meant to evoke a public response.

Specialized and Unusual Prayers

Over the centuries, a number of specialized and unusual prayers have been written and used by people in a variety of situations. Here is a sampling.

ANCIENT PRAYERS

Prayer for the Journey

This prayer, to be said when traveling or taking a trip, has its source in the Talmud (*Berachot* 29b):

> May it be Your will, O Lord our God and God of our ancestors, to lead us toward peace, to direct us toward peace, and make us reach our desired destination for life, gladness, and peace. Deliver us from every enemy, conflict, and hurt that we may encounter along the way, and from all painful afflictions that trouble the world.

Bless all that we do; grant us Your divine grace, kindness, and mercy in Your eyes and in the eyes of those that we meet. Listen to the voice of our appeal, for You are a God Who responds to pleas and prayers. Praised are You, O Lord, who hearkens to prayer.

The Bedtime Shema

This prayer is to be recited upon retiring. It has, as one of its sources, the talmudic Tractate *Berachot* 60b:

Blessed are You, O Lord, Sovereign of the universe, who closes my eyes in sleep and my eyelids in slumber. May it be Your desire, God of my ancestors, to grant that I lie down in peace and that I rise up in peace. Let not my thoughts upset me, nor evil dreams. May my family be perfect in Your sight. Grant me light, lest I sleep the sleep of death. It is You Who gives light to the eyes. Praised are You, O Lord, whose majesty gives light to the entire world.

Blessing the Sun

The rabbis taught that a person who sees the sun at its turning point, the moon in its power, the planets in their orbits, or the signs of the zodiac in their order should recite, "Blessed are You Who make the work of Creation." This opportunity occurs every twenty-eight years or when the signs of the zodiac in their orderly progress begin again, says Abaye (*Berachot* 59b).

The blessing of the sun (*Birchat Hachamah*) is a prayer service in which the sun is blessed in thanksgiving for its being created and set into motion in the firmament on the fourth day of Creation. The ceremony itself takes place once every twenty-eight years, after the *Shacharit* service, when the sun is about ninety degrees above the eastern horizon, on the first Wednesday of the month of Nisan. First, participants recite Psalms 84:12, 75:5, and 75:2, Malachi 3:20, Psalms 97:6, and Psalm 148. This is followed by the blessing: *Baruch ata Adonai Elohaynu melech ha'olam oseh ma'asey v'resheet* ("Blessed are You, O Lord our God, Source of Creation"). Next, Psalms 19 and 121 are read, followed by the hymn *El Adon*. The ritual ends with a thanksgiving prayer in which the community thanks God for sustaining it.

Note: The Jewish community blessed the sun on April 8, 1953, and March 18, 1981. The next blessing of the sun will occur on April 7, 2009.

Blessing the Moon

The blessing of the moon originated in the time of the Second Temple. The basic text for blessing the moon is presented in the Talmud (*Sanhedrin* 42a and *Soferim* 2:1). The prayer can be recited from the third evening after the appearance of the New Moon until the fifteenth of the lunar month. The blessing is recited because the moon, in Judaism, is seen as a symbol of both the renewal of nature and Israel's renewal and redemption. It is preferable to recite the blessing of the moon in the presence of ten persons. The moon must be clearly visible and not obscured by clouds. Here is the basic text for blessing the New Moon:

> Rabbi Yochanan said: "Whoever blesses the New Moon at the proper time is considered as having welcomed the presence of the *Shechinah*."

Halleluyah. Praise the Lord from the heavens. . . . Praise Him, angels on high. . . . Praise Him, sun and moon . . . [and] shining stars. Praise Him, highest heavens. . . . Let them praise the Name of the Lord, at Whose command they were created, at Whose command they endure forever, and by Whose laws nature abides [Psalms 148:1–6].

Blessed are You, O Lord our God, Sovereign of the universe, Whose word created the heavens, Whose breath created all that they contain. He set statutes and seasons for them, that they should not deviate from their assigned task. Happily they do the will of their Creator, Whose work is truth. He said to the moon that it should renew itself, a crown of glory for those who were borne from the womb, who are destined to be renewed and to extol their Creator for the name of His glorious sovereignty. Blessed are You, O Lord, who renews the months.

•　　•　　•

David, King of Israel, lives and endures.

Greetings are then exchanged with three different people:

Shalom aleichem—
　—Aleichem shalom.

The following is recited three times:

May a good sign and may good fortune be ours and blessing for us and for the entire House of Israel. Amen.

Family Blessings

The source of the family blessings is Numbers 6:23–26. In this section of the Bible, God speaks to Moses, who, in turn, is told to speak to his brother Aaron. God then presents Aaron with the blessing that has come to be known as the threefold Priestly Blessing.

Today it is customary for parents to bless their children before sitting down to enjoy the Sabbath evening meal. In the touch of a parent's hands or the sound of a parent's voice, children often feel and respond to the love and affection their parents have for them. The blessing for boys invokes the shining example of Jacob's grandchildren, Ephraim and Menasseh, who, although raised in Egypt, maintained their identity as Jews. The blessing for girls refers to the four Matriarchs, Sarah, Rebekkah, Rachel, and Leah, all of whom were known for their concern for others.

Here is the family blessing for both boys and girls:

For boys, parents gently place both hands on his head and recite:

Yesimcha Elohim k'Efraim v'chi'Menasseh.
May God make you like Ephraim and Menasseh [Genesis 48:20].

For girls, parents approach each daughter and gently place both their hands upon her head and recite:

Yesimaych Elohim k'Sarah, Rivka, Rachel, v'Leah.
May God make you like Sarah, Rebekkah, Rachel, and Leah.

For both boys and girls, the benediction concludes with the Priestly Blessing.

Yevarechecha Adonai v'yishmerecha.
May the Lord bless you and guard you.

Ya'er Adonai panav aylecha vichuneka.
May the Lord shine His countenance on you and be
gracious to you.

Yisa Adonai panav aylecha veyaseym lecha shalom.
May the Lord turn His face toward you and grant you
peace.

Maimonides's Oath for Physicians

When physicians are ready to begin their medical practice, they take an oath. The Hippocratic Oath has, for
centuries, been the standard vow. The Medical Oath of
Maimonides is often chosen by Jewish doctors, and is
now being used in some medical schools as well.

> Your eternal Providence has appointed me to watch over
> the life and health of Your creatures. May the love for my
> art actuate me at all times, may neither avarice nor
> miserliness, nor thirst for glory or for a great reputation
> engage my mind, for the enemies of truth and philan-
> thropy may easily deceive me and make me forgetful of
> my lofty aim of doing good to Your children.
>
> May I never see in the patient anything but a fellow
> creature in pain.
>
> Grant me strength, time, and opportunity always to
> correct what I have acquired, always to extend its
> domain, for knowledge is immense and the spirit of man
> can extend indefinitely to enrich itself daily with new
> requirements.
>
> Today he can discover his errors of yesterday, and
> tomorrow he can obtain a new light on what he thinks
> himself sure of today. O God, You have appointed me to
> watch over the life and death of Your creatures. Here I

am, ready for my vocation, and now I turn unto my
calling.

Prayer for the Amelioration of a Bad Dream

One who has had a disturbing dream can perform the
following prayer ritual the next morning with three
willing friends. The passages in bold type are recited by
the dreamer; the other passages are recited in unison by
the dreamer's three friends.

Do not interpretations belong to God? Tell it to me, if you
please. Recite seven times: **I have seen a good dream.**
You have seen a good dream. It is good, and may it
become good. May the Merciful One transform it to the
good. May it be decreed upon it seven times from
heaven that it become good and always be good. It is
good, and may it become good.

**You have changed for me my lament into dancing.
You undid my sackcloth and girded me with gladness.** Then the maiden shall rejoice in a dance, and lads
and elders together. And I shall change their mourning to
joy, and I shall console them and make them happy from
their sorrow. The Lord your God did not wish to pay
heed to Bilaam; the Lord your God transformed for you
the curse to blessing, for the Lord your God loves you.

**He redeemed my soul in peace from the battles that
were upon me, for the sake of the multitudes who
were with me.** And the people said to Saul, "Shall
Jonathan die who performed this great salvation for
Israel? A sacrilege—as God lives, if a hair of his head
falls to the ground, for with God has he acted this day."

And the people redeemed Jonathan, and he did not die. Those redeemed by God will return and arrive at Zion with glad song and gladness on their heads. Joy and happiness shall they attain, and sorrow and groan shall flee.

I create fruit of the lips: Peace, peace, for far and near, says God, and I shall heal him. A spirit clothed Amitai, head of the officers: "For your sake, David, and to be with you, son of Jesse, peace, peace to you, and peace to him who helps you, for your God has helped you." David accepted them and appointed them heads of the band. And you shall say, "So may it be as long as you live, peace for you, peace for your household and peace for all that is with you. The Lord will give might to his people, and the Lord will bless His people with peace."

God, I heard what you made me hear and I was frightened. God during these years, give him life. God, during these years, make known amid rage and remember to be merciful. **A song to the ascents. I raise my eyes to the mountains, whence will come my help. My help is from the Lord, Maker of heaven and earth.** He will not allow your foot to falter. Your Guardian will not sleep. The Guardian of Israel, God is your Shade at your right hand. By day the sun will not harm you, nor the moon by night. God will protect you from every evil. God will guard your soul, your departure and your arrival, from this time and forever.

God spoke to Moses saying: Speak to Aaron and his sons, saying: So are you to bless the children of Israel, say to them: May the Lord bless you and guard you. May the Lord shine His countenance upon you and be gracious to you. May the Lord turn His countenance toward you and grant you peace. Let them place My Name upon the children of Israel, and I will bless them.

May You reveal to me the path of life. The fullness of joys in Your Presence, there is delight at your right hand for eternity. Recite once: Go with joy, eat your bread, and drink your wine with a glad heart, for God has already approved your deeds. And repentance, prayer, and charity remove the severity of the decree. And peace be upon us and upon all Israel, amen.

God's Prayer

Rabbi Yochanan said in the name of Rabbi Yossi . . . "God, the Holy One, Blessed be He, prays . . . What is God's prayer?"

Rabbi Zutra says in the name of Rav [God prays as follows]: "May it be My will that My mercy overcome My anger, and My loving qualities override My strict traits; that I treat My children with the quality of mercy and that I always deal with them beyond the letter of the law" (*Berachot* 7a).

Shortest Biblical Prayer

In Numbers, Moses offers this short prayer on behalf of his sister Miriam, who has been stricken with the dreaded disease of leprosy: *El nah, refah nah lah* ("God, please heal her!").

Prayer Recited upon Recovery from a Serious Illness

The following benediction is recited by one, or on behalf of one, who has recovered from a serious illness, returned safely from a long journey, or survived any type of danger (including childbirth). It is generally recited upon being called to the Torah for an *aliyah*.

Baruch ata Adonai Eloheinu melech ha-olam ha-gomel lechayavim tovot she-g'malini kol tov.
Blessed are You, O Lord our God, Sovereign of the universe, Who graciously bestows favor upon the deserving, even as He has bestowed favor upon me.

The congregation responds:

Mi she-g'malcha [she-g'malech, for a woman] kol tov, hu yig'molcha [yigm'lech, for a woman] kol tov selah.
May God who has been gracious to you continue to favor you with all that is good.

Blessing upon Seeing 600,000 or More Jews Together

Baruch ata Adonai Eloheinu melech ha-olam chacham harazim.
Blessed are You, O Lord our God, Ruler of the universe, Knower of secrets.

Prayers Said Immediately Following the Conclusion of the *Amidah*

Today, the prayer recited immediately upon concluding the *Amidah* is that of Mar, son of Ravina, called *Elohai*

Netzor "O God, guard my tongue from evil . . . ." The following is a selection of prayers with which talmudic rabbis concluded their recitation of the *Amidah*.

1. When Rabbi Eleazar concluded his *tefillah*, he would add: "May it be Your will, O Lord our God, that in our lot there reside love and fellowship, peace and friendship. May you make our territories abundant in students. To the very end of our lives, may You endow us with hope and expectation. Set our portion in paradise. May You sustain us in Your world with a good friend and good impulse. When we get up in the morning, may we find hearts yearning to fear Your Name, and may You be pleased to regard our contentment with favor" (*Berachot* 16b).

2. When Rabbi Yochanan concluded his *tefillah*, he would say: "May it be Your will, O Lord our God, when seeing our shame and glimpsing our evil plight, to clothe Yourself in Your compassion, wrap Yourself in Your kindness, gird Yourself with Your graciousness, and have the attribute of Your kindness and gentleness come into Your presence" (*Berachot* 16b).

3. When Rabbi Zeira finished his *tefillah*, he would add: "May it be Your will, O Lord our God, that we do not sin, so that we need not feel shame or disgrace in the presence of our forebears" (*Berachot* 16b).

4. When Rabbi Chiyya concluded his *tefillah*, he would say: "May it be Your will, O Lord our God, that Your Torah be our occupation, and that, as we study it, our hearts do not ache nor our eyes grow faint" (*Berachot* 16b).

5. When Rav finished his *tefillah*, he would add: "May it be Your will, O Lord our God, to grant us a long life, a life of peace, a life of goodness, a life of blessing, a life of sustenance, a life of bodily vigor, a life in which there is fear of transgression, a life free from shame and embarrassment, a life of sufficiency and honor, a life imbued by love of Torah and fear of heaven, a life in which You will fulfill all the wishes in our hearts that are good for us" (*Berachot* 16b).

6. When Rabbi concluded his *tefillah*, he would say: "May it be Your will, O Lord our God and the God of our ancestors, to deliver us from the arrogant and from arrogance, from an evil person, from evil fortune, from the impulse to evil, from an evil friend, from an evil neighbor, from the destructive accuser, and from a difficult lawsuit and adversary in the suit, whether he be a son of the covenant or not" (*Berachot* 16b).

7. When Rabbi Safra concluded his *tefillah*, he would add: "May it be Your will, O Lord our God, to establish peace in the household above and in the household below, as well as among the students who immerse themselves in Your Torah, whether they do it for its own sake or not. May it be Your will that all who study Torah not for its own sake will come to study it for its own sake" (*Berachot* 17a).

8. When Rabbi Alexandri concluded his *tefillah*, he would add: "May it be Your will, O Lord our God, to put us in a corner where there is light and not darkness, and let not our hearts ache or our eyes grow cloudy." According to some, this was the prayer

of Rabbi Hamnuna, but when Rabbi Alexandri concluded his *tefillah*, he would continue: "Sovereign of the universe, it is known and apparent to You that our intention is to do Your will. But what is it that hinders us? The leaven in the dough and the servitude to the foreign kingdoms. May it be Your will that, both in front of us and behind us, You subdue them both, so that we may return to do the ordinances of Your will with our whole heart" (*Berachot* 17a).

9. When Rava concluded his *tefillah*, he would add: "My God, before I was formed, I was of no value, and now that I have been formed, it is as though I had not been formed. I am but dust while alive; how much the more so when I am dead. I stand before You as a vessel filled with disgrace and bewilderment. May it be Your will, O Lord my God, that I sin no more. And the sins that I have committed before You, wipe them away in your great mercy, though not by means of suffering or aching diseases" (*Berachot* 17a).

Prayer Said When Traveling in a Dangerous Place

The following talmudic prayer was recited by Rabbi Joshua when he would travel in a dangerous place.

Rabbi Joshua said: "One who is traveling in a dangerous place may entreat God in a short prayer, saying, 'Deliver, O God, your people, the remnant of Israel. On every crossroads, may their needs be before You. Blessed are You, O Lord, Who hears prayer'" (*Berachot* 28b).

Prayer Said upon Seeing a Friend After a Lapse of over Twelve Months

Friendship was highly valued in talmudic times, and friends saw each other with great frequency. If a friend had not seen his friend for a year, it was a likely sign that his friend had died. Thus developed this prayer, which appears in the Talmud:

Blessed be God Who revives the dead (*Berachot* 58b).

Prayer upon Seeing Jewish Graves

Blessed be God Who fashioned you in justice, Who maintained you in justice, fed you in justice, and in justice gathered you in, and in justice will raise you up again (*Berachot* 58b).

Prayer Said When Death Is Imminent (*Vidui*)

O God and God of my ancestors, accept my prayer and do not reject my supplication. Forgive me for all of the transgressions that I have committed during my life. I am ashamed and abashed for all of the wrong things that I have done. Accept my pain and suffering as an atonement and forgive my transgressions, for only against You have I sinned.

May it be Your desire, O Lord my God and the God of my ancestors, that I transgress no more. With Your great mercy, cleanse my sins, but not through suffering and pain. Send a total healing to me and to all those who are afflicted.

I acknowledge to You, O Lord my God and the God of my ancestors, that my life is in Your hands. May it be

Your will to heal me, but if You have decreed that I shall not recover from my sickness, I accept the decree from Your hand. May my death make amends for all the sins and all the transgressions that I have committed before You. Shelter me in the shadow of Your wings and grant me a portion in the World-to-Come.

Father of all orphans and Guardian of widows, be with me and protect my dear family, for my soul is bound up with theirs.

Into Your hand do I commit my spirit. You have redeemed me, O Lord, O God of truth.

Hear O Israel, the Lord is our God, the Lord is One.

Prayer Recited before Retiring at Night (The Bedtime Shema)

Blessed are You, O Lord, Sovereign of the universe, Who closes my eyes in sleep and my eyelids in slumber. May it be Your desire, God of my ancestors, to grant that I lie down in peace and that I rise up in peace. Let my thoughts not upset me, nor evil dreams. May my family be perfect in Your sight. Grant me light, lest I sleep the sleep of death. Blessed are You, O Lord, whose majesty gives light to the entire world.

Hear O Israel, the Lord is our God, the Lord is One. Blessed be the Lord's majestic reputation forever and ever. Love the Lord with all you heart, soul, and might. And these words which I command you today shall be in your heart. Teach them carefully to your children, and speak of them when you sit in your home, when you go on a journey, when you lie down and when you arise. Bind them as a sign on your arm and they shall be for frontlets between your eyes. Inscribe them on the doorposts of your house and on your gates (Deuteronomy 4:6–9).

Prayer for Eating *Chametz*

During the Passover of 1944, there was no *matzah* (unleavened bread) at the Bergen-Belsen concentration camp. The rabbis would not permit the inmates to endanger their lives by fasting, and they decreed that it was permissible for them to eat bread, provided the following prayer was recited before meals:

Avinu Shebashamayim [our Father in heaven], it is evident and known to you that it is our desire to do Your will and to celebrate the Passover Festival by eating *matzah* and by observing the prohibition of leavened food. But our heart is pained that the enslavement prevents us, and we are in danger of our lives. We are, therefore, prepared and ready to fulfill Your commandment: "And you shall live by my commandments, and not die by them."

We pray to You that You may keep us alive and preserve us and redeem us hastily so that we may observe Your laws and do Your will and serve You with a perfect heart. Amen.

Techinot

A *techinah* is a supplicatory prayer, usually said quietly, whose subject is often the relationship between God and the people of Israel. In addition to those in Hebrew, Yiddish-German *techinot* for women were published in small brochures from the beginning of the eighteenth century in Prague, Switzerland, Germany, and many towns of Russia and Poland. Occasionally, *techinot* were included as appendixes to editions of various prayerbooks. Following are two examples of this genre of personalized prayer.

A Childless Woman's Lament

My God and the God of my ancestors. You have created me from clay and given me a soul, a life in this world, and everything with great mercy. But You have made me into a vessel that, unfortunately, is somewhat useless since I have not been blessed with children. How bitter my life is! I am like a full-grown tree that bears no fruit. A great sorrow rests upon me and there is no one to share it with. I beg heaven and earth to lament on my behalf because my years slip away like [a trail of] smoke. Still, I don't blame the world for my sorrow. Should I not come [to You] with my great sins, seeking forgiveness, so that I may [at least] merit the World-to-Come?

Woe is my life! Tears flow from my eyes: How mournful is my heart! I cannot be happy. I lament and bemoan my years and the day I was born. What can I speak or say? . . . Who can heal my woe and set aright my bitter life?

You have shown me much lovingkindness and compassion. You have raised me, though I am useless. . . . Consider my sad life, dear God, and forgive me my sins. If I do not merit the blessings of this world, then at least let me be worthy of the World-to-Come so that my soul will not be ashamed there.

Master of the Universe, I must talk out my bitter heart before You. By whom am I to be offended? Whom shall I blame? My mother, who dressed herself and made herself attractive to my father so that I might be born? Her intention was for the sake of heaven, to do Your will so that the world would not be an empty wasteland, but populated. Shall I blame the bad *mazel* [luck, fate, constellation] under which I was born? All the fates must do Your bidding, for all the hosts of the heavens bow down to You and obey Your orders. . . . Shall I blame the midwife? Maybe she failed to straighten out my limbs. Shall I fault the angel who oversees pregnancies? No, each one performed his and her role to which he or she was assigned by You. They fulfilled their roles and saw to it that I was properly created to serve You and bear children [in order] to increase [life] in the world.

It is God's will because of my many sins that I am so completely alone. I cannot be angry at anyone, only at myself, for having sinned. How sad is my heart! The waters have covered my house!

I look about me and see no one but You, my Creator, to whom I can turn. I shall place myself and my soul in Your hand when my time will come. Receive me with great compassion and mercy. Accept my confessions and my hot tears with which I bemoan the day of my birth. Deliver my soul from severe decree and from *Gehinnom*. May it [my soul] be protected from Satan and find eternal shelter under Your wing. Amen.

Deliverance from Bad Neighbors

Creator of the world, You have made Your world so that man should inhabit it. I am going out now to look for a dwelling in which to settle with my husband and children. Please help me, God, send me to a nice, appropriate place where I shall not have to haggle about the rent or fall in among bad neighbors. Our Sages say: ["Keep far from a bad neighbor"] so that he may not corrupt my character; all the more so, from a neighbor corrupted in his faith, so that he may not infect my children with heresy, nor mislead my daughters into lewdness, debauchery, and profligacy. Help me get to know good, religious neighbors and learn good qualities from them. As our Sages say: ["What is a good way to which a man should cling? . . . Rabbi Jose says: 'A good neighbor.'"]

May we also be found worthy of dwelling in our own land in our own houses, quickly and in our own time. Amen.

MORE RECENT PRAYER COMPOSITIONS

Prayer Recited by Health-Care Provider in the Presence of a Patient Who Has Died

May it be Your Will, O God,

To grant eternal rest and peace
To the soul of _____ who has now surrendered life.

Help him/her pass gently into the World-to-Come
And shelter him/her with Your love.

Help me bring Your comforting presence to family and
    friends
Who need strength in this hour of pain and loss.
O God, open my heart that I may grieve this loss.
I truly cared for_____;
I mourn his/her passing.

Give me strength
That I may continue my efforts
On behalf of others who are under my care,
And help me grow in wisdom and judgment.
As I dedicate myself to enhancing life,
Let me humbly accept
That there is a time
We must each let go of living.

Adonai natan v'adaon lakach
Yehi Shem Adonai mevorach.

The Eternal has given, the Eternal has taken back;
Blessed be the Eternal.

Shema Yisrael, Adonai eloheynu Adonai echad.

(*Wrestling with Angel: Jewish Insights on Death and Mourning*, edited by Jack Riemer (Schocken Books, New York, 1995), pp. 79–80).

Twentieth-Century Prayer of Shmuel

Shmuel was a boy who celebrated an improvised bar mitzvah ceremony in a displaced persons' camp in Germany after the Holocaust (see Nahum Glatzer, *The Language of Faith,* p. 78).

I pray that my mother and father may look from heaven and see that their son is a bar mitzvah today, and they may know that my sister and I have remained good Jews, and will always remain so.

NOTABLE PRAYER QUOTATIONS

PRAYER WITH PROPER CONCENTRATION
AND DEVOTION

Rabbinic advice states that, before engaging in prayer, the worshipper ought to assume a proper devotional frame of mind in order for the prayers to be said with feeling. The Hebrew term *kavanah* (literally meaning "direction") was the word that they used to describe this correct intention. The following quotations relate to the theme of proper devotion in prayer and how one prepares oneself for the prayer experience.

1. Prayer without devotion is not prayer. . . . The person whose thoughts are wandering or occupied with other things ought not to pray. . . . Before engaging in prayer, the worshipper ought to bring himself into a devotional frame of mind, and then he

must pray quietly and with feeling, not like one who, carrying a load, unloads it and departs (Maimonides, *Yad*, Tefillah 4:16).

2. If you are not at peace with the world, your prayer will not be heard. Forget everybody and everything during your prayers; forget yourself and your needs; forget the people of whom you have need (Rabbi Nachman of Bratzlav).

3. The person who prays must direct his heart to heaven (*Berachot* 31a).

4. One should not pray in a place where, or at such a time when, there is interference with *kavanah* (Orach Chayyim 98:2).

5. One stands up to pray only when in a reverent frame of mind (*Berachot* 5:1).

6. The Holy One, blessed be He, desires the heart (*Sanhedrin* 106b).

7. One whose mind is not at ease should not pray (*Eruvin* 65a).

8. The pious men of old used to wait an hour before they said their prayers, that they might direct their hearts toward God (*Berachot* 5:1).

9. Prayer is service of the heart (*Taanit* 2).

10. Prayer without intention is like a body without a soul (*Yeshuot Meshicho*).

11. A person must purify his heart before he prays (Exodus Rabbah, Beshallach 22:3).

12. Rabbi Eliazar said: "Always let a person test himself:

If he can direct his heart, let him pray; if he cannot, let him not pray" (*Berachot* 30b).

13. If a person is riding on a donkey [and the time for prayer arrives], if there is anyone who can hold his donkey, let him get off and pray. If not, let him remain on the donkey and pray. Rabbi said: "In either case, let him remain on the donkey and pray. The most important thing is that his heart should be directed" (*Berachot* 3:18).

14. A load carrier, even when the burden is on his shoulders, may recite the Shema. But while he is either putting on or taking off the load, he may not recite it, because he cannot direct his heart (*Berachot* 2:7).

15. Rabbi Joshua ben Levi said: "When a person is about to begin praying, he should sit down twice—once before he begins, and once again afterwards. Beforehand, he should recite, 'Happy are they who sit in Your house, they are forever praising you' [Psalms 84:5]. Afterwards, he should recite, 'The righteous shall certainly praise Your name, the upright shall sit in Your presence'" [Psalms 140:14] (Jerusalem Talmud, *Berachot* 5:1).

16. The person whose prayers are answered is the person who lifts his hands with his heart in them (*Taanit* 8a).

17. The person who stands in prayer will keep his eyes down and his heart upward (*Yevamot* 105).

18. Just as it was necessary that the beast intended for sacrifice be without blemish in order to prove accept-

able, so too prayer must be without a blemish, namely without foreign thoughts, in order to prove acceptable (*Zohar* Chadash Tikkunim 108b).

19. The words "to serve God with all of your heart" means to concentrate your mind upon your prayer, so that your heart be not divided in the hour of prayer (Pesikta Zutarta, Numbers 11:13).

20. Rabbi Eliezer said: "If a person prays only according to the exact words of the prayer and adds nothing from his own mind, that prayer is not proper entreatment" (*Berachot* 28).

21. Neither levity nor indolence, neither austerity nor worldliness, must be the mood in prayer, but joy springing from the very love of communication (*Berachot* 31a).

22. Rabbi Chiyya and Rabbi Simeon bar Rabbi were once sitting together when one of them began this discussion. "A man at prayer should direct his eyes toward the place here on Earth [where the Temple was located] in keeping with the scriptural verse, 'And My eyes and My heart shall be there forever'" [1 Kings 9:3].

    The other said, "He should direct his eyes upward toward the heavens, for the Torah says, 'Let us lift up our heart with our hands to God in the heavens'" [Lamentations 3:41]. In the meantime, Rabbi Ishmael, son of Rabbi Yose, joined the two of them and asked, "What is the subject under discussion?"

    "One's posture at prayer."

    Rabbi Ishmael said, "My father ruled this way: 'A person, when praying, should direct his eyes toward the place here on Earth [where the Temple had originally been located] and direct his heart toward the heavens above, in order to comply with both verses'" (*Yevamot* 105b).

23. When you pray, make your prayer not a routine, but a plea for mercy and a supplication before the Holy One, blessed be He. Rabbi Eliezer said: "When a person makes his prayer a routine, it is not supplication." What is meant by routine prayer? Rabbi Jacob bar Idi said in the name of Rabbi Hoshea: "Anyone whose prayer is but a heavy burden." The sages said: "The person who does not say it as a supplicator." Rabbah and Rabbi Joseph both said: "The person who is not able to bring something fresh into it." Abba bar Abin and Rabbi Chanina bar Avin both said: "The person who does not make an effort to pray [in the morning and the evening at the proper time], when the sun appears to stand still" (*Ethics of the Fathers* 2:13).

24. Rabbi Yose bar Chanina used to pray at the time the sun appeared to stand still [i.e., in the morning], so that the fear of Heaven might be upon him all day (Jerusalem Talmud, *Berachot* 2:1).

25. Rabbi Hezekiah said: "A person's prayer is not heard until one makes his heart soft like flesh, as it is written: 'It shall come to pass that from one new moon until another . . . all flesh shall come to worship Me' [Isaiah 66:23]" (*Sotah* 5a).

26. Rabbi Eleazer would first give a copper to a poor person and then pray, explaining that it is written,

"Through charity I shall behold Your face" [Psalms 17:15] (*Baba Batra* 10a).

27. Our rabbis taught: One should not stand up to say the *tefillah* (i.e., the *Amidah*) when depressed, when indolent, when laughing, when gossiping, when frivolous, or when engaged in idle matters, but only when still rejoicing after the performance of a *mitzvah* (*Berachot* 32a).

28. When you pray, always know before Whom you stand (*Berachot* 28b).

29. Rabbi Channah bar Bizna said in the name of Rabbi Simeon the Pious: "When a person prays, he should regard himself as though God's Presence were before him, in keeping with, 'I regard the Lord as always before me' [Psalms 16:8]" (*Sanhedrin* 22a).

30. A person should not stand on a chair, a footstool, or any place that is elevated when he says the *tefillah*, but should stand in a place that is low-lying and say it there, in keeping with the verse: "Out of the depths I called upon You, O Lord" [Psalms 130:1] (*Berachot* 10b).

31. Rabbi Hamnuna said: "How many important rulings can be derived from the verses about Hannah at prayer [1 Samuel 1:10ff]. Regarding the verse, 'Now Hannah spoke with her heart,' we learn that a person must direct his full heart toward prayer. . . . 'And Eli thought that she was drunk'—from this verse we learn that one who is drunk is forbidden to pray" (*Berachot* 31a).

32. Rabbi Iddi, son of Rabbi Simeon, said in the name of Rabbi Yochanan: "People should not pray if they

have to use the bathroom" (Jerusalem Talmud, *Berachot* 2:3).

33. A person should not stand up to pray after completing a profane conversation or a jocular exchange of words, but should rise for prayer after having finished a wise or learned conversation (Tosefta *Berachot* 3).

34. When wood burns, it is the smoke alone that rises upward, leaving the grosser elements below. So it is with prayer. The sincere intention alone ascends to heaven (The Baal Shem Tov).

THE PROPER LENGTH OF A PRAYER

In the following quotations we learn that a prayer can be long or short. Its length is not the standard by which it is judged.

1. Rabbi Meir said: "Let a person's words before God always be few, as it is written, 'Be not rash with your mouth, and let not your heart be hasty to utter a word before God. For God is in heaven, and you on earth; therefore let your words be few' [Ecclesiastes 5:1]" (*Berachot* 61a).

2. And the Lord said to Moses, "Wherefore do you cry to Me?" [Exodus 14:15]. Rabbi Eliezer said: "God said to Moses, 'My children are in trouble, the sea shuts them off on one side, the enemy chases them on the other, and you stand and recite lengthy prayers.' God said, 'There is a time to lengthen prayers, and there is a time to shorten them'" (*Mechilta*, Beshallach 3).

3. Rabbi Chiyya ben Abba said in the name of Rabbi Yochanan: "Whoever prolongs his prayer and calculates on it [i.e., anticipates reward for its length] will eventually come to pain of heart" (*Berachot* 32b).

4. Rabbi Akiba, when he prayed with the congregation, was short (*Berachot* 3:7).

5. "And he cried to God, and God showed him a tree" [Exodus 15:25]. Thus you can learn that the righteous have no difficulty in getting their prayers to be answered, and you may also learn that the prayers of the righteous are short (*Mechilta Vayetze*, Beshallach 1).

6. The rabbis point to the example of Moses, who, on one occasion, prayed for forty days and forty nights, and on another was content with a single sentence: "O God, heal her now, I beseech You" (paraphrase of *Berachot* 31a).

7. A reader went down before the Ark in the presence of Rabbi Chanina and said, "O God, great, mighty, awesome, majestic, powerful, feared, strong, overwhelming, reliable, and honored." Rabbi Chanina waited until the reader finished. When he had finished, he asked him, "Have you concluded all the prayer epithets to be accorded to your Master? Why did you have to say so many? We would not have been permitted to utter even the three we do utter, had not Moses our teacher mentioned them in the Torah and had not the men of the Great Synagogue come and included them in the *tefillah*. Yet you not only uttered the three, but you went on and on. It is as if a king of flesh and blood had a thousand gold

dinars and was praised for possessing silver ones. Would that not be an insult to him?" (*Berachot* 33b).

8. Our rabbis taught: Once a certain student went down before the Ark in the presence of Rabbi Eliezer and greatly lengthened his prayers. Rabbi Eliezer's disciples said, "Master, what a long-winded person this one is."

   Rabbi Eliezer answered, "Did he make his prayers lengthier than did our teacher Moses who mentioned the forty days and forty nights that he fell down in prayer?" [Deuteronomy 9:25].

   It happened one other time that a certain student went down before the Ark in the presence of Rabbi Eliezer and made his prayers very short. Rabbi Eliezer's students said, "What a terse person he is."

   Rabbi Eliezer answered, "Was he any more terse than our teacher Moses, who prayed, "Heal her, O God, I ask You" [Numbers 12:13] (*Berachot* 34a).

9. Rava saw Rabbi Hamnuna lengthening his prayers. He said, "Some people forsake eternal life [i.e., Torah study] and occupy themselves with temporal life." But Rabbi Hamnuna held that the time for prayer is reckoned by itself, and the time for study is reckoned by itself (*Shabbat* 10a).

10. Rabbi Joshua said: "One who is traveling in a dangerous place may entreat God in a shorter prayer, saying, "Deliver, O God, Your people, the remnant of Israel. On every crossroads, may their needs be before You. Blessed are You, O Lord, who hears prayers" (*Berachot* 28b).

THE TIME FOR PRAYER

There are many laws and customs related to the correct time for prayers. Here is a cross-section of opinions related to this theme.

1. How many times ought a person to pray? Our rabbis taught: One should not pray more than three times daily, for the three Patriarchs instituted the three statutory prayers: Abraham, the morning service [Genesis 19:27]; Isaac, the afternoon service [Genesis 24:63]; and Jacob, the evening service [Genesis 27:11] (*Tanchuma*, Mikketz 98).

2. Rabbi Jose ben Chalafta taught, There are proper times for prayer, as it says: "As for me, let my prayer come before You, O Lord, at an acceptable time" [Psalms 69:14]. What is meant by "an acceptable time"? When the community is at prayer (Tanchuma Mikketz 98b).

3. Rabbi Jose ben Chanina would pray in the morning at sunrise so that he might have upon him the fear of heaven all day (Jerusalem Talmud, *Berachot* 4).

4. Rabbi Eleazar, the son of Rabbi Simeon, said: "As soon as the sun begins to rise, one should pray, as it is written, 'They shall fear You while the sun endures'" (1 *Zohar* 178).

5. Why is not time set for prayer? Were a person to know the time when, if he prays, he will be answered, he would leave off other times and pray only then. Thus, the Holy One, blessed be He, said: "For this reason, I do not let you know when you will be answered, so

that you will be willing to pray to Me at all times," as it is written: "Put your trust in Him at all times" [Psalms 62:9] (Aggadat Bereshith 77).

6. Rabbi Joshua ben Levi said: "A person should always come early to the house of prayer, so that he may merit being counted among the first ten" (*Berachot* 47b).

FIXED VERSUS SPONTANEOUS PRAYER

Rabbinic opinion is mixed regarding the virtues of making one's prayers fixed rather than spontaneous. Here are several quotes that clearly show the admixture of rabbinic views related to the fixed, prescribed prayer versus the spontaneous, more emotional one.

1. They entered a town and found a cantor who recited, "The great, powerful, awesome, mighty, courageous God," and they silenced him, saying, "You are not allowed to add to the phrasing which the Sages have established for blessings" (Jerusalem Talmud, *Berachot* 9).

2. Rabbi Yose says: "Whoever changes the phrasing which the Sages determined for blessings has not fulfilled his obligation" (*Berachot* 40b).

3. A person reading the Shema during the morning service must include and mention the Exodus from Egypt as part of *Emet Veyatziv* (Jerusalem Talmud, *Berachot* 1:3).

4. Be careful when reciting the Shema and the *Amidah*. When you do pray, do not make your prayer rigid,

but rather compassionate and pleading before God
(*Ethics of the Fathers* 2:18).

5. If someone wants to add to each of the intermediate
blessings of the *Amidah*, that person may do so
(Maimonides, *Laws of Prayer* 6:2–3).

6. Let not your prayer be a matter of fixed routine, but
heartfelt supplication for kindness at the divine footstool (Mishnah *Berachot* 5:1).

7. Rabbi Eliezer said: "If a person prays only according
to the exact text of the prayer and adds nothing from
his own mind, that prayer is not proper imploration"
(*Berachot* 28).

8. Rabbi Acha said in the name of Rabbi Jose: "It is
necessary to add new words to the text every time the
Amidah is recited" (Jerusalem Talmud, *Berachot* 4).

9. Rabbi Acha said: "A new prayer should be said every
day" (Jerusalem Talmud, *Berachot* 4:3).

PUBLIC PRAYER VERSUS PRIVATE PRAYER

Praying with others in a community has always been a
basic feature of the Jewish prayer structure. Though an
individual is permitted to pray alone if unable to participate in a quorum of ten, the preferred situation is
communal prayer. Here are some quotations related to
the theme of community prayer versus private prayer.

1. "Why," asked Rabbi Isaac, "does the master not attend
prayer services in the synagogue?"
   "I cannot," Rabbi Nachman replied.

"Then," continued Rabbi Isaac, "why not collect a *minyan* [i.e., quorum of ten] at home?"

"That," maintained Rabbi Nachman, "would be too much trouble."

"Then," Rabbi Isaac continued, "why not ask the cantor to tell you the exact time of the congregational service, so that you can synchronize your prayers with their prayers?"

Rabbi Nachman responded, "Why all of this concern?"

"Because," replied Rabbi Isaac, "Rabbi Yochanan quoted Rabbi Simeon ben Yochai [on Psalms 69:14, "As for me, let my prayer be for You, O Lord, in an acceptable time"] as teaching: 'What time may be considered acceptable? When a congregation is at prayer'" (*Berachot* 7b–8a).

2. Prayer of the congregation is always heard by God. Even if there are sinners among them, the Holy One, blessed be He, does not reject the prayer of the congregation (Maimonides, *Laws of Prayer* 8:1).

3. Rabbi Jacob said in Rabbi Chisda's name: "Whoever goes on a journey must recite the Prayer for the Journey." What is it?

"May it be Your will, O God, to lead me in safety and direct my steps in safety. . . . Blessed are You, O Lord, who listens to prayer."

Abaye said: "One should always associate with the congregation. How, therefore, should one recite the prayer? 'May it be Your will, O God, to lead *us* to safety and direct *our* steps in safety'" (*Berachot* 29b–30a).

4. Rabbi Judah said: "Thus did Rabbi Akiba conduct himself. If he prayed in public, he would hasten with his prayer lest it be a hardship upon the public. But, if he prayed alone, he would pray long with many bowings" (*Berachot* 31).

5. Rabbi Jonah would recite the *Amidah* in the synagogue in an undertone, lest he disturb the others. But, if he prayed at home, he would recite it aloud so that his sons might learn it by hearing it from him (Jerusalem Talmud, *Berachot* 4).

6. God says: "If a person occupies himself with Torah, practices kind acts, and prays with the congregation, I will ascribe it to him as though he had redeemed Me and Israel from exile among the peoples of the world" (*Berachot* 8a).

7. God does not reject the prayer of the multitude (*Sifre Numbers*, Pinchas 135).

8. Hillel said: "Do not separate yourself from the community" (*Ethics of the Fathers* 2:5).

IMPROPER PRAYERS

Not all prayers were considered proper ones, according to the rabbis. For example, one is not allowed to pray to God for the impossible; such a prayer is classified as a "prayer in vain." Here are some quotations related to improper prayers.

1. We may not pray that an overabundance of good be removed from us (*Taanit* 22).

2. Rabbi said: "It is not permitted to pray that God send death to the wicked" (*Zohar* Chadash 105).

3. To pray for the impossible is a disgrace. It is as if a person brought into a shed a hundred measures of corn and prayed, "May it be Your will that they become two hundred."

   Thus, how should one pray? "May Your blessing enter into the corn, not Your curse" (Tosefta *Berachot* 7).

4. To pray for something that has already happened is considered a prayer uttered in vain. For instance, if a man's wife is pregnant and he says, "May it be God's will that my wife give birth to a boy," that is a prayer in vain (*Berachot* 54a).

WHICH DIRECTION TO FACE IN PRAYER, AND PROPER MODULATION OF VOICE IN PRAYER

There are a number of rabbinic quotations related to the direction that one must face during prayer as well as the use of one's voice. Today, in the western world, the custom is to face the holy city of Jerusalem (i.e., east) while praying. For this reason most Holy Arks in synagogues are designed to face in an easterly direction. (Those in other parts of the world face whichever direction is toward Jerusalem.)

1. Our rabbis taught: A blind person, or anyone who cannot direct his gaze toward a particular point of the compass, should direct his heart toward his Father in heaven. If such a person is standing outside the land

of Israel, that person should direct his heart toward the land of Israel, as it is written: "Pray unto You toward their land" [1 Kings 8:48]. If he stands in the land of Israel, he should direct his heart toward Jerusalem, as it is written: "And they pray to the Lord toward the city which You have chosen" [1 Kings 8:44]. If he is standing in Jerusalem, he should direct his heart toward the Temple, as it is written: "They pray toward this house" [2 Chronicles 6:32]. If he is standing in the Temple, he should pray toward the Holy of Holies, as it is written: "They pray toward this palace" [1 Kings 8:35]. If he is in the east, he should turn his face to the west. If in the west, he should turn his face to the east. If in the north, he should turn his face to the south, and if in the south, he should turn his face to the north. In this way, all Israelites will be turning their hearts toward the same place (*Berachot* 30a).

2. Rabbi Yochanan said in the name of Rabbi Simeon ben Yochai: "Why was it instituted that the *tefillah* be spoken in a whisper? In order not to embarrass transgressors" (*Sotah* 32b).

3. The person who makes his voice heard during his *tefillah* is of those whose faith is small. The one who raises his voice during his *tefillah* is at one with false prophets.

4. From the verse, "Channah's voice could not be heard," we learn that it is forbidden to raise one's voice during *tefillah* (*Berachot* 31a).

5. The person who makes his voice heard during prayer is of small faith. Rabbi Huna said: "This teaching

applies only to one who is able to direct his heart when whispering. But if he is unable to do so, he is permitted to pray aloud. This holds true only of one praying alone, but when praying with a congregation, it would cause a disturbance to others" (*Berachot* 24b).

TEARFUL PRAYERS

A number of references are made to prayers that are rendered with tears. Such prayers are generally considered very powerful ones. Here is a sampling of these statements.

1. Never has a tearful prayer been uttered in vain (1 *Zohar* 132b).

2. When a person in affliction sheds tears as he entreats God, his entreaties will be heard (1 *Zohar* 223a).

3. Tears break through the heavenly gates and doors (2 *Zohar* 245b).

4. Tears of entreaty and penitence, as well as tears beseeching relief, open the portals of heaven and ascend to the Sovereign of sovereigns (*Zohar*, Hadash to Ruth 80a).

5. The heart's cry to God is the highest form of prayer (2 *Zohar* 20a).

THE SYNAGOGUE

The synagogue has come to be known as the place par excellence of congregational prayer. No human institution has had a longer continuous history than the synagogue, and none had done more for the uplifting of the spirit of the Jewish people. Here are statements and quotations related to prayer and the synagogue.

1. Rabbi Chelbo said in the name of Rabbi Huna: "When a person leaves the synagogue, he should not take big steps." Abbaye added: "Only when one comes from the synagogue. But when one goes to it, it is his duty to run, as it is written, 'Let us hurry to know God' [Hosea 6:3]" (*Berachot* 6b).

2. Our rabbis taught: One is not to behave in a free-and-easy manner in synagogues. One should not eat or drink in them, make use of them for one's own pleasure, stroll about in them, or go into them on hot days in order to avoid either the heat or the rain. Nor is one allowed to deliver a eulogy for a person mourned by only a few. But one may read Torah in the synagogue, study Mishnah in them, and deliver in them a eulogy for a person mourned by many (*Megillah* 28a).

3. Rabbi Joshua ben Levi said: "The person who spits in a synagogue is as though he spat in God's eye" (*Megillah* 28b).

4. Rabbi Assi said: "A synagogue that is used for reckoning personal accounts may as well be used to keep a corpse overnight" (*Megillah* 28b).

5. Rabbi Chisda said: "One may not demolish a synagogue before another is built" (*Baba Batra* 3b).

6. "Happy is the person that listens to Me . . . determined to enter within My doors" [Proverbs 8:34]. What is the meaning of "determined to enter within My doors"? The Holy One, blessed be He, said: "When you go to pray within the synagogue, do not remain standing at the outer door to pray there. Rather, make certain to go through the door beyond the outer one" (Deuteronomy Rabbah 7:2).

7. God said to Israel: "I bade you to pray in the synagogue in your city, but if you cannot pray there, pray in your field. And if you cannot pray there, pray on your bed. And if you cannot pray there, then meditate in your heart and be still" (Pesikta Kahana 158a).

8. Better is prayer without synagogue than synagogue without prayer (Abraham Joshua Heschel, *Ruach haTefillah Be'Yisrael*).

9. Rabbi Chiyya bar Abba said in the name of Rabbi Yochanan: "One should always pray in a house that has windows, for it is said of Daniel at prayer, 'His wisdom were open in his upper chamber toward Jerusalem' [Daniel 6:11]" (*Berachot* 34b).

10. Abba Benjamin said: "A person's prayer is heard by God only in a house of prayer, for the Torah says, 'God is willing to listen to the song and the prayer' [1 Kings 8:28]. In the place where there is song, there is to be prayer" (*Berachot* 6a).

11. Ravin bar Rabbi Adda said in the name of Rabbi Isaac: "What is the proof that the Holy One, blessed

be He, is found in a house of prayer? The verse, 'God stands in the congregation of the Almighty' [Psalms 82:1]. And what is the proof that when ten people pray together, the Presence is with them? The verse, 'God stands in the congregation of the Almighty'" (*Berachot* 6b).

12. Resh Lakish said: "The person who has a house of prayer in his city and does not enter it to pray is called an evil neighbor, as it is said, 'Thus says the Lord: As for all My evil neighbors, who barely touch the inheritance which I have caused My people Israel to inherit' [Jeremiah 12:14]" (*Berachot* 8a).

OTHER NOTABLE PRAYER QUOTATIONS

1. Why is the prayer of the righteous like a rake? As the rake turns the grain from one place to another, so too the prayer of the righteous turns the attributes of God from the attribute of anger to the attribute of mercy (*Yevamot* 64a).

2. Rabbi Jochanan said: "Would that a person pray all day, for a prayer never loses its value" (Jerusalem Talmud, *Berachot* 1:1).

3. A human king can listen to two or three people at once, but he cannot listen to any more than that. God is not so, for all people may pray to God, and God listens to all of them simultaneously. A person's ears become satiated with hearing, but God's ears are never satiated with hearing (Midrash on Psalms 65:2).

4. "In the morning my prayer comes before you" [Psalms 88:14]. Rabbi Pinchas said: "The angel who is appointed to prayer waits until the Israelites in the last synagogue have completed their prayers, and then the angel takes all the prayers, and makes them into a chaplet, and places it upon the head of God, as it says, 'Blessings are upon the head of the just,' that is to say, upon God who is the life of the worlds, who lives eternally [Proverbs 10:6]" (Midrash on Psalms 85:4).

5. Simon the Just said: "In his prayer a person should think that the *Shechinah* is before him" (*Sanhedrin* 22a).

6. Rabbi Judah ben Shalom said: "If a poor person comes, and pleads before another, that other does not listen to him. If a rich man comes, he listens to and receives him immediately. God does not behave in such a manner. All are equal before God—women, slaves, rich, and poor" (Exodus Rabbah 21:4).

7. Rabbi Pinchas, Rabbi Levi, and Rabbi Jochanan in the name of Rabbi Menachem of Galilee said: "In the time to come, all other sacrifices will cease, but the sacrifice of thanksgiving will not cease. All other prayers will cease, but thanksgiving will not cease" (Leviticus Rabbah, Tzav 9:7).

8. Rav said: "Whoever has it in his power to pray on behalf of his neighbor and fails to do so, that person is called a sinner" (*Berachot* 12b).

9. The rabbis teach: When Israel is in trouble, and one among them separates himself, the two angels of the

Service who accompany a man lay their hands on his head, and say, "This person, who has separated himself from the community, shall not see its consolation." And it is taught: If the community is in trouble, a person must not say, "I will go to my house and eat and drink, and peace shall be with you, O my soul." But a person must share in the trouble of the community, even as Moses did. The person who shares in its troubles is worthy to see its consolation (*Taanit* 11a).

10. Rabbi Chama bar Chanina said: "If a person sees that he prays and is not answered, he should pray again, for the Bible states, 'Wait for the Lord; be strong and let your heart take courage. Wait for the Lord' [Psalms 27:14]" (*Berachot* 32b).

11. Both Rabbi Yochanan and Rabbi Eleazar said: "Even if a sharp sword is actually resting on a person's neck, he should not hold himself back from praying for God's mercy" (*Berachot* 10a).

12. Rabbi Zeira said: "A person may have a favorite who so beseeches him with his needs and his wants that the person comes to dislike him and tries to avoid him. But with the Holy One, blessed be He, it is not so. The more a person beseeches God with his needs and his wants, the more God loves that person, as it is said: 'Call unto Me, and I will answer you' [Jeremiah 33:3]" (Midrashim Tehillim 4:3).

13. A person upon whom a calamity has fallen should always make it known to the public, so that many people may entreat God's mercy for him (*Chullin* 78a).

14. The person who prays to God for mercy while he himself is in need of the same thing will be answered first, for it is written, "God changed the fortune of Job when he prayed for his friends" [Job 42:10] (*Baba Kamma* 92a).

15. When a person does not distribute his tithes in generous fistfuls, his prayer will not ascend to the heaven (Numbers Rabbah 12:11).

16. Rabbi Judah said: "Repentance effects half of the atonement while prayer effects all of it" (Leviticus Rabbah 10:5).

17. Even if a person is greeted by the king while praying, that person may not return the greeting. And even if a snake is wound around his heel, he may not interrupt his prayer (*Berachot* 30b).

18. A person who belches or yawns during his prayer is of the arrogant. Some say it shows that he is vulgar. It is a bad omen for a person if he sneezes during prayer. When a person spits during his prayer, it is as if he spat in the face of the king (*Berachot* 24b).

19. Rabbi Chelbo said in the name of Rabbi Huna: "The person who sets a fixed place for his prayer has the God of Abraham as his helper. . . . What is the proof that our father Abraham fixed a set place for his prayer? The verse states, 'Abraham got up early in the morning to the place where he stood before the Lord' [Genesis 19:27]" (*Berachot* 6b).

20. A covenant has been made that the thirteen attributes of God, when recited in prayer, do not return empty (*Rosh Hashanah* 17).

21. Let others rely on the arm of flesh; Israel's weapon is prayer (Yalkut to Genesis 27:22).

22. Rabbi Abahu said: "Prayer is dearer to God than all good works and all good sacrifices" (Tanchuma Buber, Ki Tavo 1).

23. If you are not at peace with the world, your prayer will not be heard (Rabbi Nachman of Bratzlav).

PRAYER GLOSSARY

Adon Olam: A medieval prayer that generally concludes the worship service, proclaiming God's eternity and Oneness.

Aleynu: Literally, "It is incumbent upon us" . . . to praise God. It is part of the liturgy recited toward the end of each service, prior to Kaddish, in which God's universal power and the particularism of the Jewish people, as well as the covenant that binds us, are articulated.

Aliyah: Meaning literally "going up," this refers to going to the *bimah* in order to recite the Torah blessings.

Amen: "So be it"—a verbal affirmation of that which is articulated in a prayer or blessing.

Amidah: Literally "the standing prayer," this is also known as *Hatefillah* ("the prayer par excellence") because the liturgy is built around it. It is also called *Shemoneh Esrei* because it originally had eighteen blessings.

Aron haKodesh: The Holy Ark used to store Torah scrolls in the synagogue.

Arvit: Evening worship service, as designated by Sephardic Jews.

Avinu Malkeynu: Literally "Our Father, our King," this is a well-known selection from the High-Holy-Day liturgy that acknowledges God's sovereignty over the world.

Avnet: The Belt that holds the Torah scroll together while it is stored in the Holy Ark.

Ba'al Koreh: One who reads publicly from the Torah during the worship service.

Ba'al Tefillah: One who reads the liturgy during the worship service. Sometimes called the *shaliach tzibbur.*

Ba'al Tekiah: One who blows the *shofar.*

Bakashot: Petitions, particularly in the form of prayer.

Beit Haknesset: Literally "house of assembly," this is another name for the synagogue.

Beit Hamidrash: Literally "house of study," this is another name for the synagogue, especially when used for study.

Berachah: A blessing that has the specific technical formula of *Baruch ata Adonai* ("Blessed is the Lord").

Bimah: Literally "high place," it is the raised platform or pulpit in the front of the synagogue sanctuary.

Birkat HaGomel: A prayer said upon recovering from an illness or from some great danger.

Birkat HaMitzvot: A blessing recited for the privilege of performing a religious obligation.

Birkat Hoda'ah: A blessing of petition, praise, or thanksgiving.

Birkot Nehenim: These blessings persuade us to take nothing for granted, for they help us to acknowledge the beauty of the world and that which sustains us, such as food and wonders of nature.

Cantor: In Hebrew, *chazzan*. One who chants the liturgy.

Chatzi **Kaddish:** Literally Half Kaddish, a transitional prayer of sanctification.

Choshen: The breastplate placed over the Torah, reminiscent of the one worn by the priest during Temple times.

Crown: *Keter Torah* in Hebrew, it is placed on the top of the wooden Torah handles as an adornment.

Daven: To pray; the traditional Jewish posture of prayer.

Duchanen: During a worship service, those of the priestly lineage gather before the congregation to bless the people.

Erev Shabbat: The evening of the Sabbath—Friday evening.

Gabbai: A lay person in a synagogue who typically is responsible for keeping things in ritual order, particularly during the service itself.

Gelilah: The honor of dressing the Torah after it has been read.

Hagbah: The honor of raising the Torah scroll and showing it to the congregation after it has been read.

Hakafot: Synagogue processionals.

Hallel: A series of psalms (113 to 118) of praise recited on special holidays, including Chanukah, Passover, Rosh Chodesh, Sukkot, Simchat Torah, and Shavuot.

High Holy Days: Rosh Hashanah and Yom Kippur.

Kaddish: A prayer of affirmation of faith. There are five different types of Kaddish.

Kaddish *D'Itchaddata:* The "burial Kaddish," said

only at the grave immediately after the burial. It includes a paragraph that refers to the resurrection of the dead.

Kaddish *D'Rabbanan:* Literally "Rabbi's Kaddish," this is used as an epilogue to the study of rabbinic texts, containing a prayer for the welfare of all students of the Torah.

Kaddish *Shalem:* Literally "Whole Kaddish," this includes the prayer requesting God to accept all of the reciter's heartfelt prayers.

Kaddish *Yatom:* Literally the "orphans'" or "mourners'" Kaddish, it is recited for the first year after burial.

Kavanah: One's heartfelt direction (literally, "intention") in prayer.

Kedushah: The sanctification in the liturgy, "Holy, holy, holy is the Lord of Hosts, the whole world is filled with His glory."

Ken Yehi Ratzon: A liturgical response to the Priestly Blessing, meaning "May it be Your will."

Kerovah: A specialized liturgical poem.

Keter Torah: A crown-like ornament for the Torah.

Keva: Meaning "fixed," this refers to those prayers that are fixed in word or time by Jewish law or custom.

Kiddush: The sanctification prayer over wine for the Sabbath and specific Jewish holidays.

Kiddush Levanah: A prayer upon the occasion of the renewal of the moon.

Kipah: Hebrew for head covering or skullcap. It is also known as a *yarmulke.*

Kittel: A white, robelike garment worn by some men during the High Holy Days.

Kohen: One of the class of Jewish priests, traditionally considered to be descended directly from Aaron.

Kol Nidre: Meaning "all vows," this refers to both the opening prayer chant and the evening of Yom Kippur, the Day of Atonement. The prayer asks for release from all unkept vows made during the year.

Lecha Dodi: A mystical prayer, recited on Friday evening, that speaks of the Sabbath as a bride.

Levi: A social class distinction (and tribe) in ancient Israel, used to designate assistant priests with certain responsibilities in the Temple.

Ma'ariv: The evening worship service.

Machzor: A holiday prayerbook.

Malchuyot: Literally "sovereignty," this refers to the section of the *Amidah* during the *Musaf* service recited on the High Holy Days, acknowledging God's sovereignty in the world.

Mechitzah: A divider used in traditional synagogues to separate the men from the women during prayer.

Me'il: The Torah mantle and covering.

Menorah: A seven-branched candelabrum used in the ancient tabernacle and Temple.

Mezuzah: Literally "doorpost," it refers to both the parchment on which portions of the Torah are written and the case in which it is placed.

Mincha: The afternoon worship service.

Minyan: The quorum of ten adults (men only, in traditional Judaism) required for the reciting of prayers limited to communal recitation.

Musaf: The additional prayer service on the Sabbath and Festivals.

Ner Tamid: The eternal light in the synagogue.

Pesukei D'Zimra: Preliminary prayers, selected mostly from Psalms.

Piyyutim: Medieval liturgical poems written for special occasions and Festivals.

Pizmon: A poem praising God. It originally referred

to the first or last line of the first stanza, a kind of refrain that was repeated.

Rimmon: Literally "pomegranate," this refers to the individual ornaments that adorn Torah scrolls.

Rosh Chodesh: The first day of the Jewish month, celebrated as a minor holiday.

Selichot: Penitential prayers.

Shacharit: The morning worship service.

Shaliach Tzibbur: Literally "messenger of the congregation," this is the one who leads the congregation in prayer.

Shamash: The synagogue beadle, known in Yiddish as the *shammos*.

Shema: A central prayer that proclaims the unity of God.

Shevarim: Three blasts of the ram's horn.

Shofar: The ram's horn.

Shofarot: Part of the *Musaf* service for Rosh Hashanah, consisting of verses related to the ram's horn.

Shuckling: A back-and-forth swaying movement in prayer, used most typically by traditional Jews and Chassidim.

Siddur: Prayerbook, from the Hebrew word for "order," because it establishes the proper order for the recitation of prayers.

Synagogue: Called *schul* in Yiddish and referring to the Temple as well, this is the central house of worship for the Jewish community.

Tallit: The prayer shawl.

Tallit Katan: A small four-cornered garment, also called *arba kanfot*, that traditional Jewish men and boys wear underneath their shirts.

Tefillah: Prayer.

Tefillin: Phylacteries, or prayerboxes, strapped to the head and arm and worn daily during morning services, except for the Sabbath and Festivals.

Tekiah: One solid blast of the ram's horn.

Teruah: Nine rapid blasts of the ram's horn.

Tzitzit: The ritual fringes on a prayer shawl, tied with special knots and intended to remind a person of the 613 commandments.

Unetaneh Tokef: A Rosh Hashanah prayer that describes the procedure on the Day of Judgment.

Wimpel: A Torah binding used to hold the scrolls together. Also called the *avnet.*

Yad: The pointer used by the reader to follow the Torah reading.

Yigdal: A medieval hymn that poetically describes Maimonides's Thirteen Principles of Faith.

For Further Reading

The following are sources for further reading on the subject of prayer.

Arian, Philip, and Azriel Eisenberg. *The Story of the Prayerbook*. Hartford: Prayer Book Press, 1968.

Arzt, Max. *Joy and Remembrance: Commentary on the Sabbath Eve Liturgy*. Bridgeport, CT: Hartmore House, 1979.

————. *Justice and Mercy*. New York: Burning Book Press, 1963.

Brown, Steven M. *Higher and Higher: Making Jewish Prayer a Part of Us*. New York: United Synagogue Department of Youth, 1979.

Donin, Hayim Halevy: *To Pray as a Jew*. New York: Basic Books, 1980.

Garfiel, Evelyn. *Service of the Heart: A Guide to the*

Jewish Prayer Book. Northvale, NJ: Jason Aronson, 1989.

Goldstein, Rose. *A Time to Pray.* Bridgeport, CT: Hartmore House, 1972.

Hertz, Joseph. *Authorized Daily Prayer Book.* New York: Bloch Publishing, 1961.

Idelsohn, A. Z. *Jewish Liturgy and Its Development.* New York: Schocken, 1975.

Kadden, Bruce, and Barbara Binder Kadden. *Teaching Tefillah.* Denver: A.R.E., 1994.

Millgram, Abraham. *Jewish Worship.* Philadelphia: Jewish Publication Society, 1971.

Munk, Elie. *The World of Jewish Prayer.* New York: Feldheim, 1961.

Petuchowski, Jakob J. *Understanding Jewish Prayer.* New York: Ktav, 1972.

Scherman, Nosson, and Meir Zlotowitz, eds. *The Siddur.* Brooklyn, NY: Mesorah Publications, 1981.

Tarnor, Norman, ed. *A Book of Jewish Women's Prayers.* Northvale, NJ: Jason Aronson, 1993.

INDEX

Vows, and *Kol Nidray*,
149–150

Wave offerings, 7
Windows, in synagogues,
48
Wine, blessings for, 83–
84, 145
Women
covering heads by,
56–57
prayerbook for, 73
techinot for, 178–180
wearing *tallit*, 58–59
World-to-Come, as the
Sabbath, 142
Writings, Books of, 154

Yarmulke. See Kipah

Yehudah, Rabbi Daniel
ben, 146
Yigdal, 145–146
Yishtabach, 116–117
Yochanan, Rabbi, 171, 173
Yom Kippur
prayers for, 149–151
use of prayer garments
on, 55, 58, 69
Yose, Rabbi, 37
Yose ben Yosen, 94
Yotzer (piyyatim), 96

Zakkai, Rabbi Yochanan
ben, 10
Zeira, Rabbi, 173
Zohar, 31, 116
Zutra, Rabbi, 171

About the Author

Rabbi Ronald H. Isaacs currently serves as spiritual leader of Temple Sholom in Bridgewater, New Jersey. He holds a doctorate in instructional technology from Columbia University. He is the author of numerous books, including *The Jewish Book of Numbers, Close Encounters: Jewish Views about God, Sacred Seasons: A Sourcebook of Holiday Legends, Becoming Jewish: A Handbook for Conversion,* and *Critical Jewish Issues.* He is the coauthor of *The How To Handbook for Jewish Living* with Kerry M. Olitzky, and *Loving Companions: Our Jewish Wedding Album* with Leora Isaacs. Rabbi Isaacs serves on the editorial board of *Shofar* magazine and on the board of the New Jersey Rabbinical Assembly. He resides in New Jersey with his wife, Leora, and their children, Keren and Zachary.